LET THE SUN IN

ALEXANDER GIRARD

LET THE SUN IN
TODD OLDHAM & KIERA COFFEE

A Way of Seeing 8

Textile Design 42

Product Design 100

Braniff International Airways 148

Detrola 166

Curation and Exhibition Design 176

Letterforms 208

Restaurants 222

La Fonda del Sol 236

Commercial Interiors 256

Residential Interiors 278

The Rieveschl Residence 294

The Miller House and Garden 304

Girard's Studios 314

Girard's Homes 334

Timeline 392

A Way of Seeing

ALEXANDER GIRARD WAS BORN ON MAY 24, 1907, in New York City, to American-born Lezlie Cutler and Italian-born Carlo Matteo Girard. The family moved from New York City to Florence, Italy, in 1909, where Alexander Girard was raised under the artistic influence of his father—a wood carver and collector of fine arts. Matteo, as he was known, shared his creative passions with all three of his children (Alexander, his brother, Tunsi, and their sister, Pezzie), and all three made artful things throughout their youth and into adulthood (for both livelihoods and passions).

By the time Girard returned to New York as a young man in 1932, he had earned two architectural degrees, one in London and one in Rome. But the United States was in the depths of the Great Depression, and more architectural firms were shuttering rather than working on projects. Girard widened his scope and began seeking interior design work. Soon, he opened his first design studio, which focused on interior design, architectural renovation, and product design. A few years later, in 1935, he got his third architectural degree from NYU, and also met his future wife, Susan Needham, a friend of his sister, Pezzie. During this time, Girard created unusually embellished and greatly admired interior designs for private clients and show houses, each rife with handmade elements that contrasted with the popular spare design style. With a solid understanding of what was important, Girard said, "The hope for good design lies in those designers who believe what they do, and who will only do what they believe."

Throughout Girard's outlandishly wide-ranging career, he revealed an unusual facility for architecture as well as interior design, graphic design, textile design, and product design. He showed the world not just his unique style in each of these arenas, but his unique style of looking at things. By creating custom graphics, furnishings, and lighting for each client, he raised questions about how frequently designers might alter accepted standards, and how they might borrow from the past without duplicating it, which Girard did beautifully. His work could flit effortlessly between chic, understated designs full of subtle color and texture (exemplified by restaurants, homes, and office interiors) and extremely vivid designs that gleamed with bright tones and patterns (an airline rebranding, many showroom designs, and textiles). The way Girard could accomplish this range without losing his recognizable style was a wonder.

After the successful start of the Girard Studio in New York City, Susan and Alexander moved west to Michigan in 1937, where an expanded studio replaced Girard's earlier one. In Michigan he took on home design projects, store redesigns, and more. He also accepted the role of chief designer at the Detrola Corporation, designing radios and turntables. Girard's unbridled enthusiasm and uninhibited mind soon had him redesigning the Detrola offices, its cafeteria, and the factory itself—none of which was included in his job description. His time at Detrola marked a turning point—from that moment on, almost every one of his projects included uncommonly large quantities of custom designs. If he designed a shelf for a client, it would be sized and shaped to hold its owner's belongings specifically; if he designed a sofa, it might discreetly house a client's stereo in its side or their book collection; if he designed a restaurant interior, he would design details as small as waitstaff uniforms and graphics for napkins and menus.

Even though Girard trained as an architect, he saw an unbreakable connection between architecture and interior design. In *Progressive Architecture* magazine, he was quoted as saying, "Since it is impossible to conceive of an architecture (a space-enclosing structure) as existing without an interior space, one cannot then think of 'interior design' or interior space as a separate activity disconnected from architecture." He fused the two, using interior design to move people comfortably through each of his spaces.

Girard's comprehensive approach to design made people examine mass-produced products in a way

P. 7 Alexander Girard at his home on Lothrop Road, Grosse Pointe, Michigan, 1949.

P. 8–9 Alexander Girard in his Grosse Pointe studio, 1940s. Photograph by Charles Eames.

← Girard in mischievous repose reading *What Is Modern Painting?*, published in 1943 by the Museum of Modern Art, New York.

→ Door and fireplace watercolor renderings, 1933. Possibly for the *Permanent Exhibition of Arts and Crafts* at Rockefeller Center, 1935.

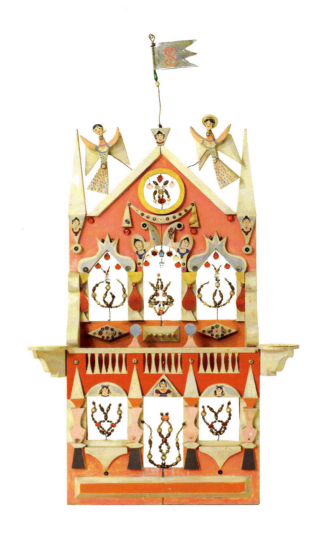

A collection of Girard's wooden sculptures, featuring the Mexican devotional charms *milagros*, beaded wire, painted wooden flowers, and plaster relief, 1940s.

they hadn't previously. Through his customizations, he specialized, personalized, and humanized first objects and then whole rooms, stores, and factories. Later in his career, he said humorously, "An interior design is really a slow-motion movie of junk changing position." But really, he cared so deeply for details that he tended to outrageous numbers of them for each client. Every Girard assignment had the discipline of total immersion behind it.

Through both his travel and work, Girard came to meet a number of fascinating characters making their own mark on the twentieth-century world of art and design. He was always intrigued by others who were working at the top of their fields, and while he certainly sought out and loved collaboration, he was also interested in celebrating other artists and designers in their own right. Georgia O'Keeffe became a close friend of the Girards upon their move to Santa Fe, and she stayed with them often when she came to town and traveled with them abroad. Eero Saarinen also became a good friend and important collaborator. While Girard and Saarinen worked together on a number of projects as early as the 1930s, their most important collaboration was on the Miller House and Garden in 1957, which still stands today as a seminal example of mid-century modern design and architecture. Then, of course, there were the Eames—both Charles and Ray—with whom the Girards became very close friends and longtime collaborators. Starting when Alexander Girard and Charles Eames met at Detrola and continuing throughout Girard's life and career, he shared a unique, mutual respect and admiration with both Charles and Ray. Not only did Girard and Eames work together frequently on their own projects but they also collaborated as colleagues during their respective tenures at Herman Miller.

By 1952 the well-established Herman Miller furniture company had sold modern furnishings for decades but had never produced its own textiles. Girard became the leader of Miller's first textile division, rounding out the talents of furniture designers George Nelson and Charles Eames. Girard applied his love of color and pattern to the vast textile line he created. He could not resist the play of colors, the exploration of a line, or new applications for fabrics. Girard designed, colored, and drew hundreds of patterns for Herman Miller's collection, many of which are still popular and available today. Girard had the ability to marry function and form with perfect grace in his fabrics. He knew, for instance, that his textile patterns, when they were used for curtains, would compact when drawn open, and so he set about making designs that were as lovely bunched together as they were flat. Every design was tremendously well-considered and included a pattern, color, or texture for every possible use.

During his career, Girard put his hand to all manner of projects: residential design, office renovations, a church mural, and an airline facelift, to name only a few. For these projects, he created thousands of designs, from the typographic treatment of a restaurant's identity to custom light bulbs to dinnerware, place mats, and beyond. Designer Charles Eames wrote to an editor at *Architectural Digest* magazine:

> Alexander Girard is interested in the quality of everything and does not hesitate to act on this interest, personally and immediately. Such action could not possibly result in a cliché; and not being a cliché demands an explanation (especially by magazines). The answer, perhaps, is in Girard's total involvement in things he touches, allowing no time barriers. Also of some significance is the fact that he is part magpie— and a Florentine one at that.

Throughout his work life, Girard's wife, Susan, was an essential key to his success. Not only did she manage all the administrative details for the business and their family, she also had impeccable taste and style. Importantly, she acted as liaison between Girard and the world—as he was always eager to get on to the next project, Susan took care of the back end and made sure he got proper credit for his work. Her precision, love, and devotion led to efficient office workings that allowed Girard to pursue his designs with a minimum of outside noise. Susan and Sandro (Girard's nickname) shared a passion for perfection.

In designing his family's homes, Girard often used them as launching pads and incubators for ideas. The thought of a fixed or finished interior design seemed foreign to Girard, and his own living spaces were in constant change, deliberately designed to respond to seasons and new ideas. In his 1948 Lothrop Road home in Grosse Pointe, Michigan, Girard bifurcated the main room with an angled divider that functioned as an ever-changing gallery wall. Sometimes, the wall displayed framed art and sculpture; at other times, it held more than fifty hanging wooden candleholders that bathed the living room in a flickering glow. Girard removed sheetrock and insulation from the back of the divider, which exposed its vertical wooden supports. In the recessed channels, he placed framed artwork. Girard would continuously revisit this concept of movable shelving in order to accommodate a changing array of art and objects.

Girard designed his first home in Santa Fe at the same time he designed a family home in Indiana for Irwin and Xenia Miller—one of many projects he did for the Millers.

↑ Hand-painted slip-cast porcelain vessels made in Italy and watercolor emblem studies, mid-1930s.

→ Girard explored the interlocking "S" initials of his nickname, Sandro, and his wife's name, Susan, multiple times over the years in many mediums. This version is gouache plywood, 1940s.

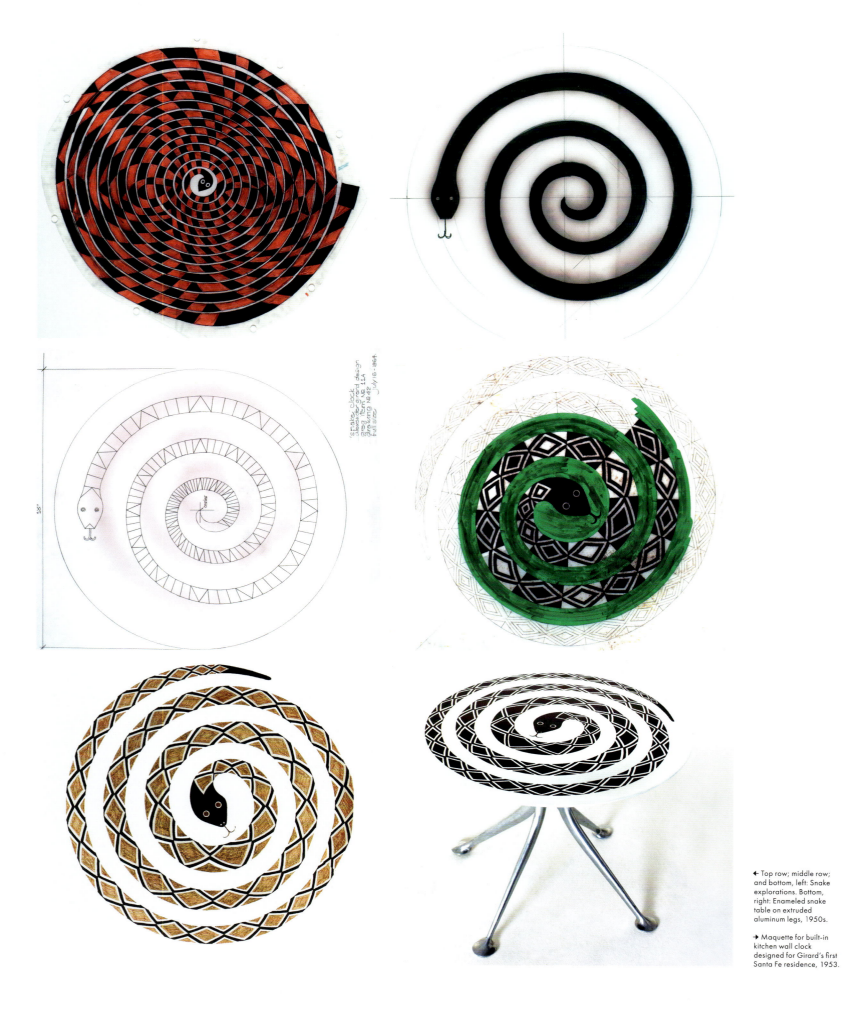

← Top row; middle row; and bottom, left: Snake explorations. Bottom, right: Enameled snake table on extruded aluminum legs, 1950s.

→ Maquette for built-in kitchen wall clock designed for Girard's first Santa Fe residence, 1953.

- Modern is not new; it is ageless honesty
- Modern of today is fifty years old
- Modern is here now, not tomorrow
- Thought + Reason = Modern
- Good modern makes sense; it's not a tricky fad
- There is a right material for every use
- A good thing has its place wherever it is useful
- Modern is "your" way of life, not that of an early settler, Spanish grandee, English manor, or French château

In his notes, Girard filtered his ideas into sections. Some were titled "Romance and Magic," "Fashion and Style," "Space, and Tradition" but his category "Morals and Honesty" feels prophetic today and reads like an instructional manual for a healthful spirit, thoughtful design, and newness. It includes good life lessons like

- Let's believe in ourselves
- Don't live in the past!
- Let's wake up to our day!
- Let yourself live!
- Let a thing be honestly itself
- Make the most of today
- Let the Sun In.

Girard's influence remains an inspiring, ferocious force in the world of design. His ability to endlessly evolve while remaining true to his singular design ethos remains a beacon today, as does his unique, otherworldly color sense and soothsayer-like ability to introduce designs decades before they existed in the zeitgeist. Girard's appreciation of the connective tissue between cultures, history, and the arts has created a pathway for all of us to share in his remarkable way of seeing.

Todd Oldham

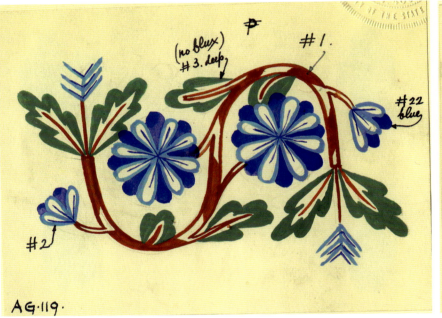

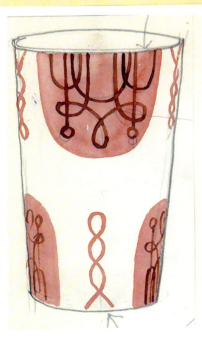

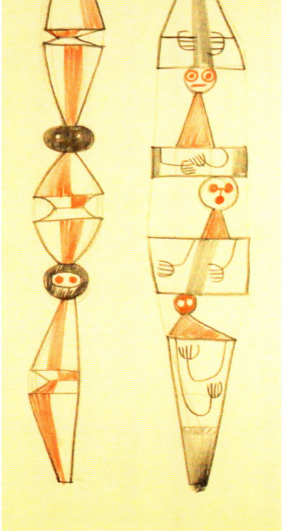

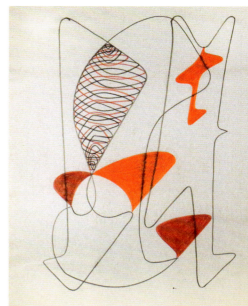

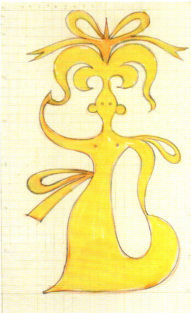

In Girard's Santa Fe home he played with his now-famous conversation pit, which held comfortable cushions, a diverse throw pillow collection, and a fur blanket. For the Millers, he designed a conversation pit as the centerpiece of their living room. He added steps down to its recessed floor and varied pillow wardrobes for winter and summer. Letters exchanged back and forth between the home's architect, Eero Saarinen, the Millers, and Girard reveal the slight challenge in convincing Xenia Miller to embrace the pit. She was concerned about sight lines from the recessed seating and wanted to avoid up-skirt views. Girard kindly built a full-scale test version in one of the Irwin Miller factories, which convinced Xenia. The Miller House and Garden became a masterwork and was later landmarked, yet Girard never repeated himself—every collaboration with Irwin Miller featured unexpected and fresh results. The dramatic Cummins Engine Co. office that Girard designed for Miller was remarkable, as was Girard's reconsideration of the Millers' hometown of Columbus, Indiana, where he designed new paint color schemes for the *entire city*.

In the 1940s through the 1950s, alongside many parallel projects, Girard entered exhibition design and curation. He created several modern design exhibitions, including *An Exhibition for Modern Living* at the Detroit Institute of Arts (1949) and *Good Design* at the Museum of Modern Art (MoMA) in New York City (1954). In each of these endeavors, he helped translate modern, sometimes foreign design concepts to public viewers. Lighting was very important to Girard, and in all his exhibition design, he created schemes that managed to cast rare, full, shadowless light. While exploring his approach to designing and curating *An Exhibition for Modern Living*, Girard created a checklist of attributes that defined the facets of modernity:

- Be honest with your home
- Don't disguise your home
- Look for the honest thing, not the "cute"
- Modern is a way of living, not a "style"

P. 18 Cityscape made for Jack Lenor Larsen, paint and marker drawing on cardboard panels, 1950s.

P. 19–22 Girard's sketchbook pages, gouache, watercolor, and colored pencil, 1930–1950s.

↑ Driftwood sculptures, gouache on driftwood, 1940s.

24 A WAY OF SEEING

← Hand-painted patterns on slip-cast Italian porcelain with gold leaf details and lathed wooden lids, 9" tall, 1930s.

→ Assorted plate drawings and finished dinner plates, made in Italy, 1930s.

← Articulated wooden figures with movable pieces, gouache on 1/4" plywood, 1940s. Girard made dozens of characters exploring daily village life, biblical events, and even his dog, Brownie (second row, middle).

↑ Left: Kinetic wooden construction, gouache on 1/4" plywood with cut steel and springs, 1940s. Right: Study for kinetic wooden construction, colored pencil on vellum, 1940s.

Wooden dolls, acrylic paint on wood, 1952. Two dolls have feathers and two wear twine necklaces. The same year, Girard purchased a new band saw, which facilitated his creation of a quirky, unusually shaped and patterned community.

← Drawings for triplets, quintuplets, and sextuplets to be made in wood, colored pencil on vellum, 1940s.

→ Abstract painting, gouache on construction paper, 1930s.

30 A WAY OF SEEING

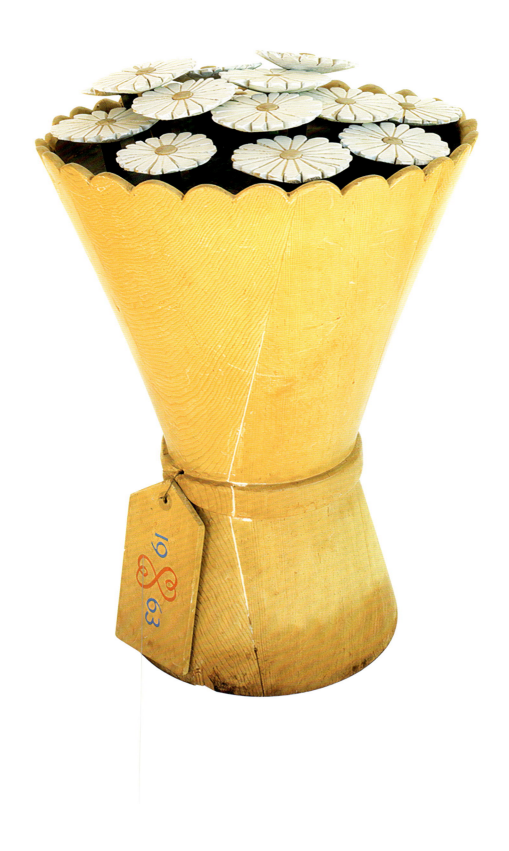

↑ Carved wooden bouquet made for Susan, 1940s.

→ Mixed media construction, painted screws and log, approx. 10" tall, 1940s.

32 A WAY OF SEEING

34   A WAY OF SEEING

← Painted wooden constructions made from a variety of materials, including reclaimed wood, gouache on found wood, and occasionally metal roofing nails. See top right in situ, page 377.

→ Paper tape and printed paper collages by Alexander Girard, 1940s.

↑ Alexander lying in Susan's lap wearing a shirt made from his textile design, *Spines*, 1930s. Also pictured, clockwise from left: Charles Eames, unknown woman, Edgar Kaufmann Jr., and Ray Eames.

→ The Girards, clockwise from right: Alexander, Sansi, Susan, and Marshall among pieces from the Girard collections, 1952. Photograph by Ezra Stoller.

← Georgia O'Keeffe, New Mexico, 1950s. Georgia O'Keeffe was a dear family friend of the Girards and often accompanied them on trips. O'Keeffe painted miniature paintings of flowers many years later for Alexander Girard's epic installation at the Museum of International Folk Art in Santa Fe. Photograph by Alexander Girard.

→ Top: I. M. Pei flanked by Susan and Alexander Girard standing in the Herman Miller Textiles & Objects shop, New York City, 1961. Middle: Ray Eames and Girard at a lunch counter, 1940s. Bottom: Girard with Charles Eames and studio assistant in Santa Fe, New Mexico, 1960s.

← Interlocking Sandro and Susan "S" form with hearts, cotton embroidery on hot pink silk shantung, 1940s.

→ Girard and cat, from a promotional shoot for Herman Miller, Santa Fe, New Mexico, 1950s. Photograph by Charles Eames.

Textile Design

IT IS UNUSUAL FOR ANY FABRIC DESIGNER to possess three architectural degrees, as Alexander Girard did. By the time he created a textile collection for Herman Miller, he had for years designed occasional fabrics for interior design clients as well as a limited collection for Knoll— both to flesh out his vision and to cover a dearth in the textile market. He said, "One of the reasons I got into the textiles was that there weren't any, and designers were always borrowing textiles or buying them from odd sources to use in their own showroom[s], just to complete the furniture." He recalled: "There was always the problem of where you get a magenta fabric, for instance—there was no such thing."

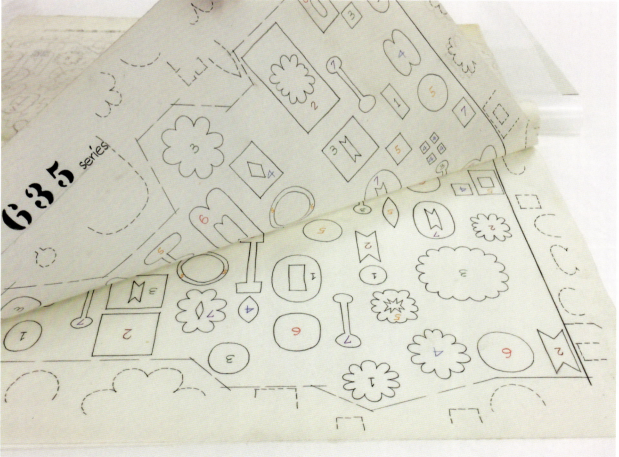

P. 42–43 Flat and bunched fabric test photo of *Multiform*, seven-color print, with scale ruler, 1954. Photographs by Charles Eames.

← Top: Hand-cut tissue paper collage for *Multiform*. Bottom: Blueprint for *Multiform*, 1954. Girard would often make multiple versions of the same print in different mediums as he developed his design.

→ *Multiform* on mustard colored basecloth, 1954.

Girard's friend, the designer Charles Eames, who had started working with Herman Miller to distribute his bent plywood furniture a few years earlier, was keenly aware of this lack of interesting textiles. After seeing what Girard was capable of when he essentially redesigned the Detrola Factory interiors (see pages 169 and 172–75), Eames knew he would be the perfect designer to bring new textiles to the fore, and in 1952 Girard was hired to lead Herman Miller's first textile division. Girard introduced brightly colored wools of the sort he had struggled to find. He added modern stripes, checks, and solids. Not all of Girard's fabrics were vividly colored; many were in charming neutrals—Girard was a strong devotee of both camps. Girard was not only interested in the color and pattern of a textile but also in its material and actual construction. He explored all of these aspects in depth and created what would become one of the most diverse collections of textiles in the twentieth century by a single designer.

The community of furniture and interior designers embraced Girard's textiles instantly. He knew their needs firsthand, and his versatile designs broadened their landscapes. The *New York Herald Tribune* wrote, "When an architect designs fabric, anything can happen." A year after his initial textile launch, Girard introduced a second line of fabrics for Herman Miller, expanding the collection. The *New York Times* wrote, "Here again brilliant rather than muted colors is a key to their success ... *Brocade* is the word, if you want to be technical. But any resemblance between them and the stuff of eighteenth-century France is so slight only a weaver would notice it."

Despite having a long, multi-hyphenate career, Girard became better known for his textile designs than almost anything else he did. Approaching their development with the draftsmanship of an architect, Girard was able to create unique and intricate patterns. Girard said, "Fabrics are a building material ... They are as much a part of a room as are the conventional materials of brick, glass, wood, and plaster." He felt textiles were integral to any room design, and he had long studied how they spoke to other design elements. He noticed when, for instance, the ruching of a curtain created too much or just the right amount of visual noise. When Girard created his textile named *Manhattan* in 1958, he kept this issue of ruching in mind. Laid flat, *Manhattan* was an uncomplicated abstraction of high rises, a series of stacked squares and rectangles

← Top: Tissue paper collage for *Ribbons*, six-color print, 1957. Bottom: Orange, red, and purple colorway of *Ribbons*, 1957. Girard would often print with pigments with a slight transparency that created new colors when overprinted and layered. The moss-colored rectangles are created by overlapping orange and purple.

→ Top: *Crosses*, six-color print, 1957. Bottom: Blueprint for *Crosses*, 1957.

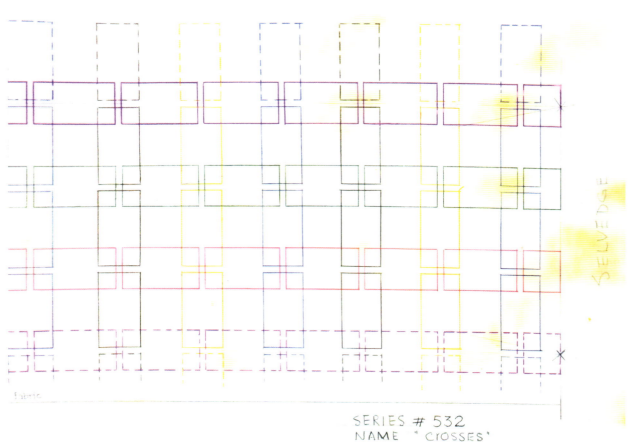

SERIES # 532
NAME "Crosses"

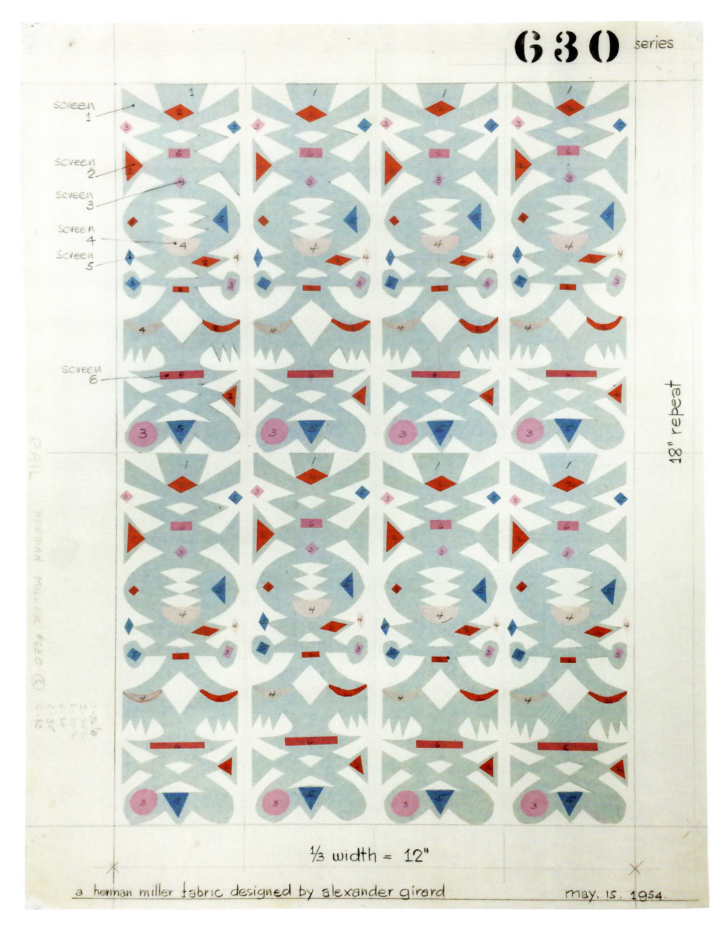

← Collage for *Arabesque*, four-color print, 1954.

→ Left: *Arabesque*, ruched and flat, 1954. Right: Three colorways of *Arabesque*, 1954. Photographs by Charles Eames.

Exploration sketches of repeating patterns, colored pencil on vellum, mid-1950s.

50 TEXTILE DESIGN

printed in pale colors (to mimic lit windows) on dark backgrounds. When the textile was gathered (as it would be for any window treatment), the small shapes overlapped intriguingly.

Over the years as Girard continued to expand his textile collection for Herman Miller, he played with tone and scale merrily, indefatigably. He could fiddle with the proportion and coloration of a striped pattern for a decade and still find fresh incarnations. He was quoted in *Retailing Daily*, saying, "There is no end to the mood of any simple geometric form." This attitude manifested in Girard being able to rearrange squares in subtle ways that altered their character profoundly. He once said, "A square is a square. It's like a basic raw material—like a tube of paint." There was magic in what Girard seemed to do very easily. Fellow textile designer Jack Lenor Larsen wrote of Girard, "His endless variations on related stripes, checks, and solids—primarily within the confines of one weave, one yarn, and one density—prove his innovative powers." Girard designed textiles briefly for the furniture company Knoll from 1947 to 1951 and consistently for Herman Miller from 1952 to 1973. His Herman Miller collection came to include every material, texture, and type of pattern one could imagine—geometrics in endless iterations, stylized florals, quatrefoils, typographic patterns, figurative and abstract repeats, stripes, plaids, dots, and of course checker. Over twenty-one years, Girard designed more than three hundred textiles for Herman Miller.

In keeping with the innovation and artistry Girard brought to his textile designs, he also found original ways to share them with prospective clients. Though unusual for a textile designer, he designed his own swatch books. There were a number of different versions to accommodate the various textiles. With elegant graphics on the covers and unique structures depending on what aspect of the textile Girard was trying to highlight, these presentations were wholly unique. One had an origami-like structure that unfolded to show the textiles in a collection together. Another was a double-sided loose-leaf three-ring binder, to make the different textiles easy to extract. Perhaps the most interesting for the time were the cards he made to showcase sheers that had a strategically placed cutout so a client could experience how light would interact with the textile.

Girard's involvement in the presentation of his textiles went beyond swatch books. Being an established display designer before, during, and after his time at Herman Miller, he was able to help showcase his textiles and took on the design of many showrooms where his fabrics were displayed. His execution in these spaces was sure-handed, and he found innovative ways to place textiles in dense arrangements that did not overwhelm the viewer.

One of the best-known of these was in San Francisco, where in 1958, Girard helped convince Herman Miller to appropriate an old Victorian music hall/ex-brothel as its showroom (see pages 54–55).

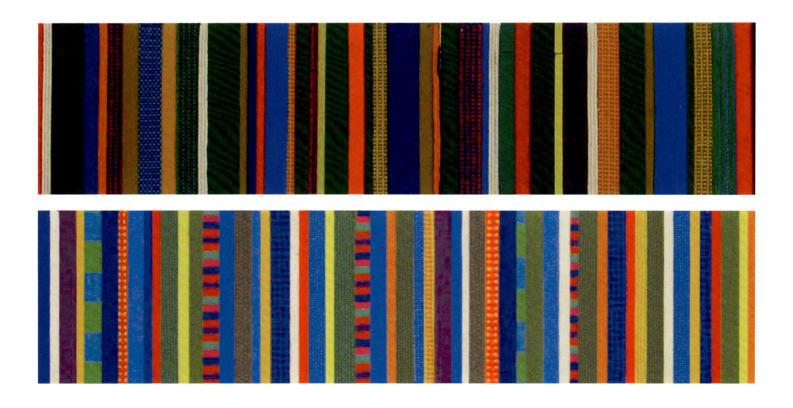

← Stripe studies for woven wool textiles made by gluing down a mix of small stripes cut from other Girard textiles, 1950s.

→ Installation images of a Herman Miller exhibition featuring swaths of Girard's textiles and Environmental Enrichment Panels stitched together into a long banner measuring more than one hundred feet long, 1970s.

54 TEXTILE DESIGN

← Herman Miller's San Francisco showroom, 1958. The Victorian building in the Tenderloin district seemed an odd choice for a modernist Herman Miller showroom, but Girard's design combined new and old ideas to create an unexpected hybrid.

↑ The Girards at the opening of the Herman Miller San Francisco showroom, 1958. Photograph by Charles Eames.

↑ Girard not only designed the textiles for Herman Miller, he also designed the swatch books, such as this one from the 1950s, that allowed the customer to flip through the book and see patterns in proximity to each other. This double-sided spiral binding was a novelty at the time.

→ For a promotional mailer for the 1955 Herman Miller textiles collection, Girard designed an unfurling origami-like stack of folding squares printed with different patterns on each side.

From the collection of fabrics and wallpapers designed by Alexander Girard for Herman Miller.

60 TEXTILE DESIGN

P. 58 Tissue paper collage of *Pins*, four-color print, 1950s.

P. 59 Girard in front of a tissue paper collage featuring marbled papers, foiled papers, and photographic cutouts, created for an exhibition titled *Space for an Open Mind*, Grand Rapids Furniture Museum, Michigan, 1951.

← Left: Colorways of *Mikado*, three-color print. Right: *Mikado*, ruched and flat, 1954. Photographs by Charles Eames.

→ Top: *Rain*, five-color print, 1953. Bottom: *Grid*, five-color print, 1958.

P. 62 *Names*, single-color print on cotton ground, 1957, containing abstracted names of Herman Miller employees.

P. 63 *Sansusie*, single-color print, 1955. This study represents one of many designs that Girard explored with interlocking "S" shapes from his and his wife Susan's initials.

← *Eden* ruched, eight-color print, 1966.

→ Multiple colorways of *Eden*, 1966.

← Multiple colorways of *January*, single-color print, 1963.

→ *January* in grass green and light blue colorways, 1963.

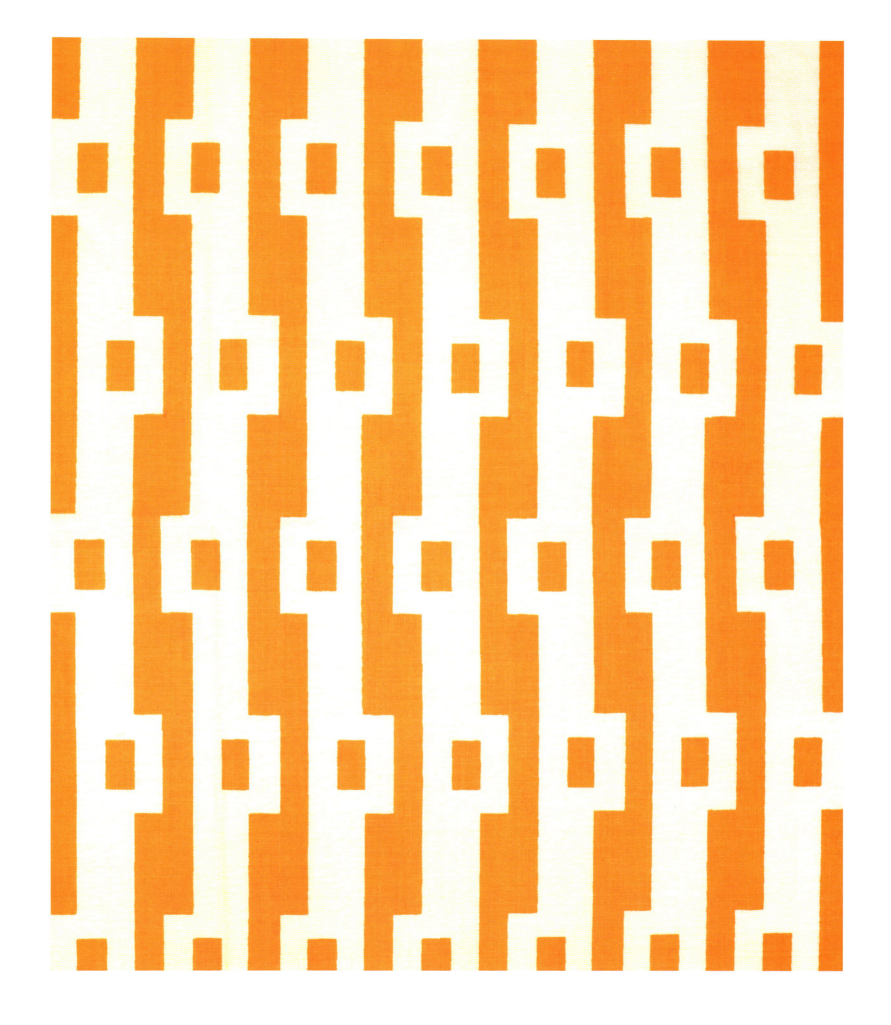

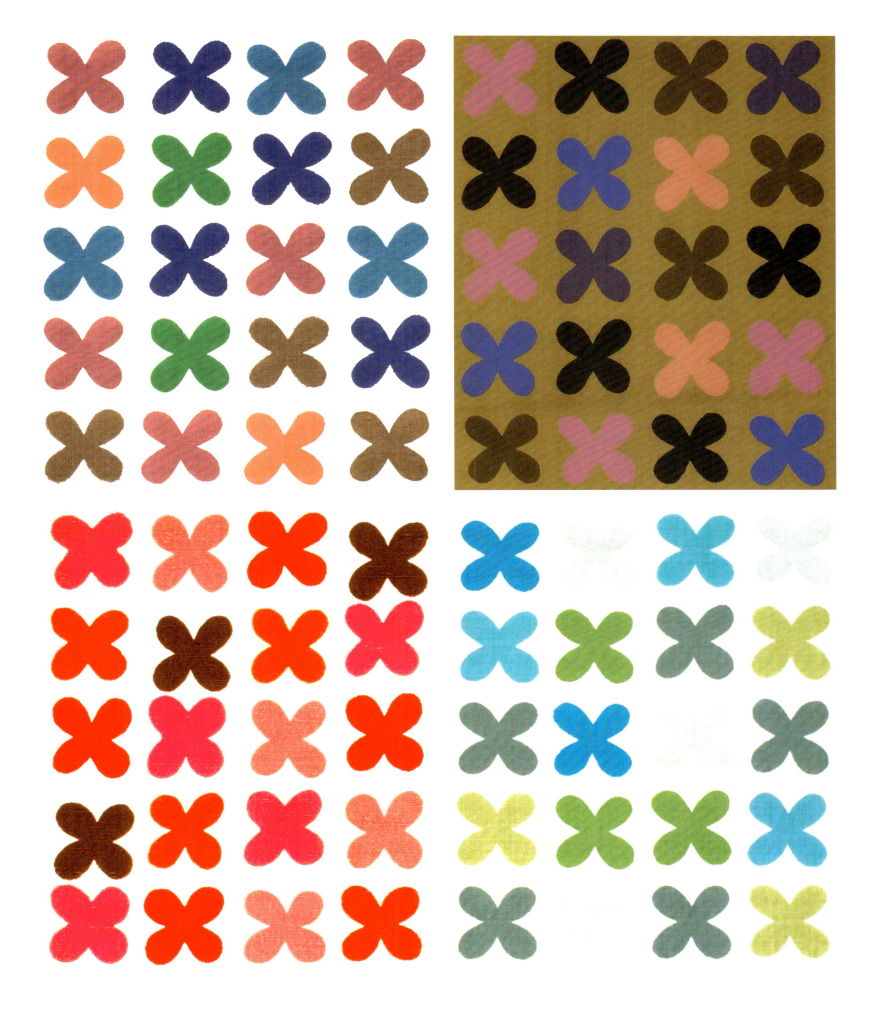

P. 68 *Firecracker*, single-color print, 1964. Girard made dramatic use of this textile when installing tall curtains in the Cummins Engine Co. office in Columbus, Indiana.

P. 69 *Jags*, single-color print, 1964.

P. 70 *Quatrefoil*, ruched, six-color print, 1954. Photograph by Charles Eames.

P. 71 Multiple colorways of *Quatrefoil*, 1954. Girard offered an unusual option for this pattern by using metallic inks mixed with the flat inks that added visual dimension.

← Multiple colorways of *Feathers*, five-color print, 1957.

→ *Feathers*, five-color print of mustard, gold, turmeric, olive, and kelly green, 1957.

P. 74 *Alphabet*, single-color print, 1957.

P. 75 Multiple colorways of *Alphabet*, 1957. There were more than twenty-one colorways available.

P. 76–77 *Super Stripe*, five-color print, 1955.

↑ *Palio*, a bold, nonrepeating eight-color print, 54" wide, 1964.

Girard's personal swatches of his woven wool stripes developed in Italy, 1960s.

P. 82–83 Girard particularly excelled at nontraditional color combinations, as evidenced in his Italian-made wool sateen stripe collections from the 1960s.

P. 84 Girard's *Mexicotton Stripes* were handwoven using traditional spinning and weaving methods that had been used for centuries in Mexico.

P. 85 Girard's classic *Checkers* pattern was woven in many colorways in 1965 and appeared across many projects, including Braniff International Airways (1965) and the Girard Group (1967).

← Drying yarns at the factory in Uruapan, Mexico, where *Mexicotton* was made, 1960s. Photograph by Alexander Girard.

P. 87–90 Girard's nonrepeating *Mexicotton Stripes* combinations in multiple colors, 54" wide, 1961.

P. 91 Top: The wooden spinning wheel used to prepare the weaving yarns for the production of *Mexicotton*, 1960s. Bottom: Girard's *Mexicotton* swatches at the factory in Uruapan, Mexico, 1960. Photographs by Alexander Girard.

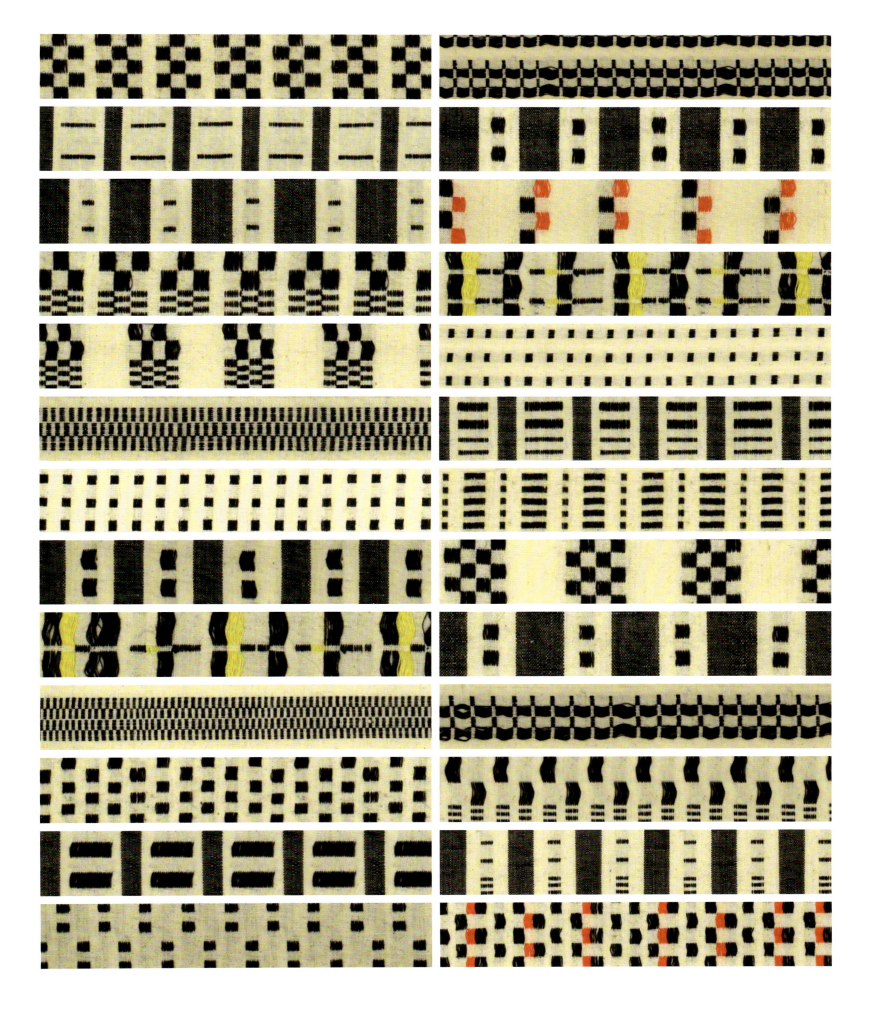

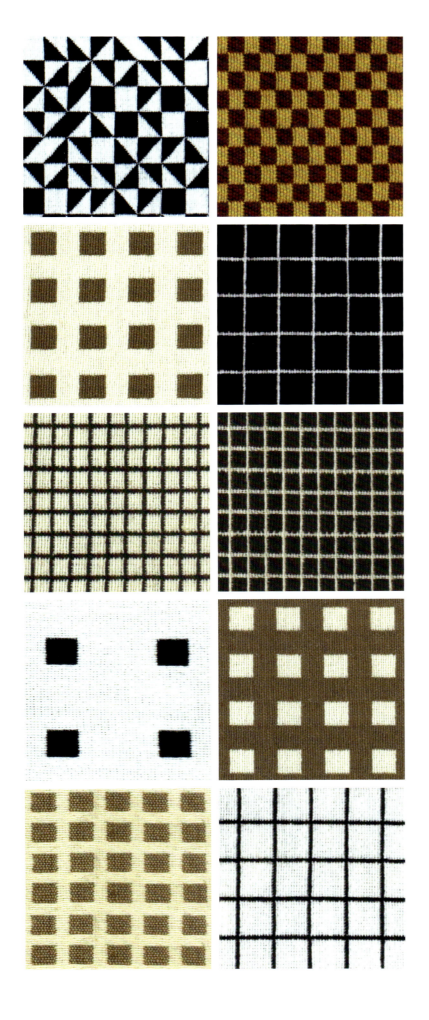

The building was ornate, hardly in sync with Herman Miller's clean, modern aesthetic. A reporter wrote at the time, "Alexander Girard transforms a den of iniquity into Herman Miller's new San Francisco showroom ... It is barely a three-minute stroll from the Herman Miller Furniture Company's former San Francisco showroom ... but psychologically the distance is enormous." *Pacific Architect and Builder* magazine observed, "Turning a bawdy Barbary Coast music hall into a furniture showroom ordinarily would be accomplished by liberal use of the battering ram and crowbar."

Girard did not subscribe to this manner of thinking. He reframed many elements of the ornate building but did not remove all of its particulars. He kept some very unmodern details, such as the gold leaf adorning the exterior of the building. He added his own modern counterpoints inside: his own chic wooden cabinets along one wall and a tall storage piece made of crisp, colorful squares (also his design) that he used as a room divider. Girard utilized a flamboyantly colored and mirrored carousel already present in the space by displaying spare Herman Miller furniture on it. The carousel, with all its detail, contrasted the furniture beautifully. Girard added charming bulbous decorations to the carousel's top, which were made from painted toilet floats. He then hung his Herman Miller textiles artfully. One reporter wrote that visitors were "pre-disarmed by the thoroughly un–Herman Millerish display of levity." Girard understood that it was not necessary to use only modern elements to display modern furnishings. (By contrast, a few years later, in 1961, he designed a stylishly modern Herman Miller showroom in New York City.) Jack Lenor Larsen wrote, "Alexander Girard is one of the greatest colorists, pattern givers, environmental and exhibition designers of our time. These media—his joy in them and ours—is his message." Because of his curatorial prowess and expert understanding of exhibition design, Girard elevated the promotion of his textiles and helped Herman Miller succeed with them.

Given the technology that did not exist in the years when Girard was designing textiles, he created his patterns in a predictably hands-on way. Each textile had its own architectural blueprint, which included not only a complex and often large repeat but also color codes, weaving, material, and specific print instructions. Inspiration for a fabric could be found anywhere: the treads of a tire left in frozen ground, the biblical story of Eden, tissue paper collages,

P. 92 Assorted geometric Mexicotton handloom swatches, two- and three-color weavings, 1960s.

← *Miller Metric* collection in elegant two-tone combinations, 1974.

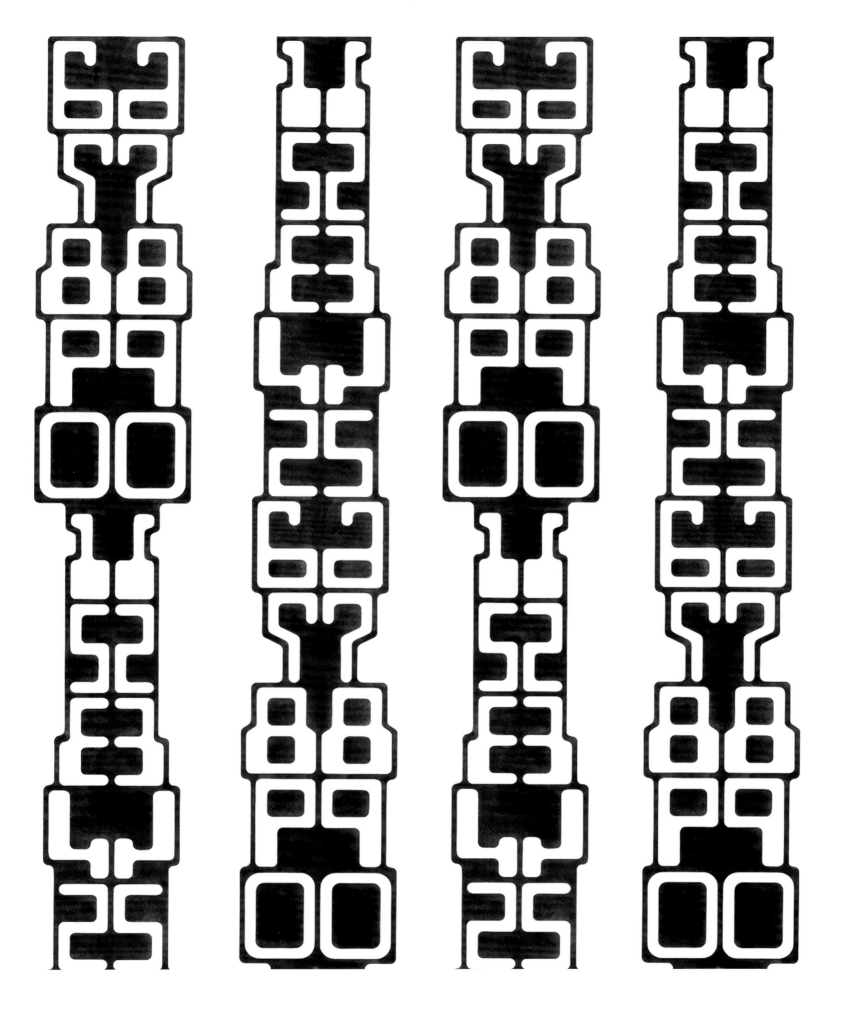

P. 94 Cut paper collage for undeveloped three-color pattern, 1950s.

P. 95 *Computer*, 1966. This pattern was strangely prophetic, as it used number forms that reference computers and flip clocks that were not common until decades later.

← *Treads*, single-color print, 1962.

→ Top, left: *Extrusion*, two-color print, 1962. Top, right: *Lace*, single-color print, 1962. Bottom: *Jagged*, single-color print, 1962.

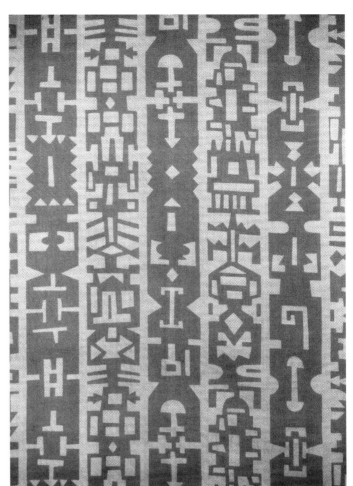

and the many textiles Girard collected from his travels throughout Central and South America, Europe, Asia, Africa, and, of course, America. When studying his visual archive, it becomes clear that he explored the potential for pattern in every possible medium, from sketches in colored pencil to watercolor renderings to tissue collages and potato stamps.

The textile called *Computer*, on which he arranged numbers from his own computer-like typeface into stripes, was inexplicably futuristic (see page 95). The design might seem unremarkable now, until one realizes he created it in 1966, when computers were not items most people had even heard of, or would have in their homes for decades. However, when one considers Girard's deep love of science fiction and his extensive knowledge of letterforms, it may make more sense. Somehow Girard tapped into it presciently, toyed with the font, and turned it into a lovely pattern.

Another of Girard's innovations shows up in nothing futuristic but its opposite—something wholly artisanal. Girard's textile *Mexicotton*, created in 1961, was handwoven and hand-dyed in Uruapan, Mexico (see pages 84–92). While fabric designers had relied on knowledgeable textile artisans in India, Scotland, and Italy for centuries, no one was gathering talent from Mexico in the 1960s. Except for Girard. He designed one *Mexicotton* stripe pattern that contained no repeating colors in its 54-inch-wide bolt. It was a far wider, nonrepeating design than anything on the market. An untrained eye might not have noticed the continually changing stripe pattern when it was used to upholster a sofa, but astute observers were enthused.

Girard was no Luddite, but he revered the handmade and, whenever possible, sought to work with artisans who had perfected their method of craft. He was excited to merge a truly ancient weaving process that hadn't been updated for centuries with his ideas of color and pattern. The *Mexicotton* collection came in stripes and checks in a large array of unusual color combinations. Due to the method of production, the hand of the fabric was uniquely textured, giving it a particularly inviting feel that made it ideal for a number of applications. As iteration was a recurrent theme for Girard, the *Mexicotton* collection also included a robust group of black-and-white geometrics that were each unique even with such constrained elements.

Girard's textile collection joyfully included many of his lifelong interests and influences while remaining versatile for others' uses. Girard naturally inserted his proclivities into everything he touched, and in this way, he was always recognizably himself. While his work looked like no one else's, it managed to complement nearly everyone's.

Top, left: *Spines*, single-color print, 1947. Top, right: *Dove*, single-color print, 1947. Bottom, left: *Links*, single-color print, 1947, produced for Knoll. Bottom, right: *Wire*, two-color print, 1949, produced for Knoll.

Product Design

DURING ALEXANDER GIRARD'S exuberantly varied career, he designed a robust number of furniture pieces and scads of covetable objects. His product designs were unanimously smart, individual, and often very colorful.

As a young architect and designer, Girard was prolific. Between 1929 and 1931, while living in Italy, he designed a chic collection of furniture and many imaginative porcelain vessels. This early furniture was largely made of wood and had spare silhouettes. One of his dressers had wide, shallow drawers and very modern pulls. Another sat on round legs made of differently hued vertical stripes of wood. He gave these striped legs to other items in his collection as well, including a side table and an octagonal dining table. (For more than three decades, he designed octagonal and hexagonal tables, landing on a hexagonal model, which featured in his 1967 Herman Miller collection.) Girard's porcelain pieces were handmade and lyrical. He painted each one himself, some with bands of 24-karat gold work. These pieces were sold in a few housewares stores in Milan.

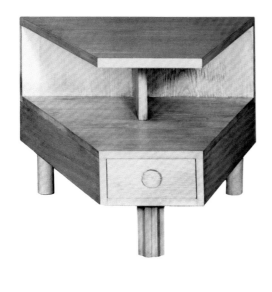

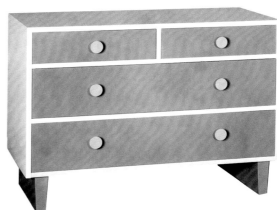

P. 100–101 Handmade wooden models for the Girard Furniture Collection, hand-carved wood, Lucite, and finishing nails painted gold, 1930s.

↑ Girard's early spare furniture designs with elegant function and surprises such as exposed plywood edges, unusual for the time, 1930s.

↑ Girard's early examinations of classic design elements, 1930s. The middle credenza features hand-forged pulls and hinges, carved tree stump legs, and a painted tree motif along with the date of the piece's creation.

← Ottoman designs, watercolor and colored pencil on vellum, 1930s.

→ Bed designs, watercolor and colored pencil on vellum and hand-printed paper, 1930s–1940s.

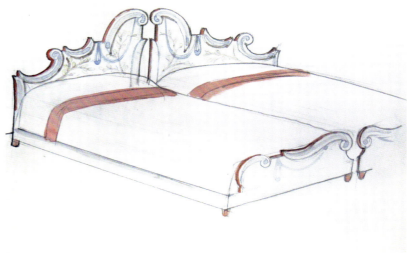
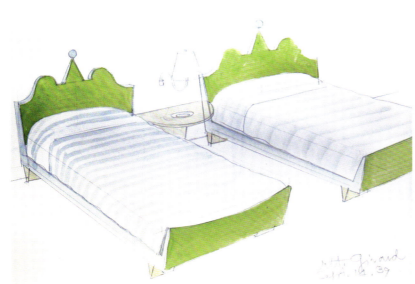

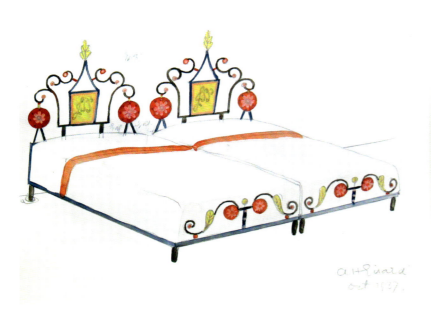
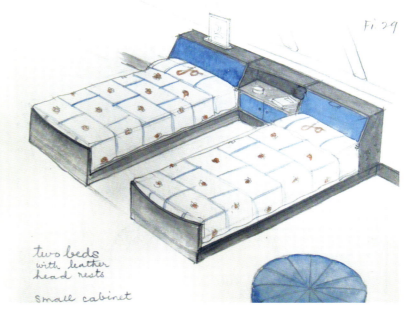

two beds with leather head rests
small cabinet

Typically, Girard's designs proved to be decades ahead of contemporary design trends. In the middle of his career, when he felt other designers could be equally inventive and predictive, he advised them to take "so-called stereotyped ideas in furniture like a tremendous grain of salt." With his focus on innovation, material exploration, and a balance between form and function, it's no accident that Girard ended up surrounded by and in collaboration with so many capable peers, including George Nelson, Charles and Ray Eames, Isamu Noguchi, Eero Saarinen, Saul Steinberg, Florence Knoll, I. M. Pei, Edgar Kaufmann Jr., and Jack Lenor Larsen.

Throughout Girard's work life, his furniture designs were primarily created for single interior design projects and private clients. As a result, the lion's share of his furnishings was never available for sale to the public. He presented countless custom-designed tables, rugs, chairs, sofas, lighting, and more to delighted clients. The scope of this would have been daunting for many other interior designers, but Girard was excited by invention and reached for it continually.

Part of what allowed Girard to deliver such a large number of customizations was the pleasure he took from blending his notions with those of his clients. This was one of the most satisfying challenges of his design work. Catching up with him in 1965, he was working on a rebranding of Braniff International Airways. As usual, once Girard fleshed out his basic schemes, he arrived at a need for distinctive furniture. He created his own—a set of elegant sofas, chairs, and stools. A year later, in 1966, Girard was working on the New York City restaurant L'Etoile when he again felt custom furniture was essential. He altered the chairs he had made for Braniff and drew a new version (in addition to many other pieces) for L'Etoile. Realizing that these chairs had potential beyond these custom projects, Herman Miller asked Girard to expand the chairs into a larger collection, which would ultimately include sofas, side tables, stools, and ottomans. Herman Miller launched this offering in 1967 as the Girard Group.

Adaptation and flexibility were integral to Girard's ethos; he had developed furniture pieces that were lightweight—pieces that people could play with and move easily to fit into a variety of rooms and arrangements. Coming out of an era when furniture was often sold in sets that matched and was too heavy to reposition without commitment, this was a new concept.

All of the furniture in the Girard Group had slim metal legs. The seating had noticeably wide arms. Everything was displayed in a large range of colors, ensuring that customers would not be limited to one upholstery color per piece. Girard said, "My theme in each case was how to make the piece flexible in color and fabric: how to make it as low and as small as possible and how to make it look not-nervous." True to the way it was displayed, Girard's "not-nervous" furniture offered an astounding number of textile options. A customer could choose one fabric for the outer portion of a sofa, one for the inner dimension, and a third for the cushions. If those weren't enough, the color of the middle welting was also up for selection. Girard had (maybe too much) faith that people knew how to play, and he felt having more options was everybody's preference. The Herman Miller press release for the Girard Group talked about its unusual number of options: "The success of the furniture in giving intense individuality to two disparate facilities led Mr. Girard and Herman Miller to believe that a collection which offered an option of more than 2,500 standard variations would solve problems in a variety of interior spaces." While this level of customization and choice was not easy for most people, there were some who took full advantage.

Girard's designs were often unusual, and he rarely stopped to worry that others might not understand or embrace them. Most of the time this worked out beautifully for him, but occasionally, a reviewer did not appreciate his originality. *House and Garden* magazine once wrote sarcastically about the dinnerware he designed for Georg Jensen, "The Girards have an aversion for sets, and believe there is nothing more tiresome than having the plates and glasses match." Girard paid little attention and kept innovating. (The debut event for that dinnerware collection, by the way, was reportedly "standing room only—or the retail store's equivalent of that phenomenon.") His especially beautiful objects spoke for themselves. Textile designer Jack Lenor Larsen said about Girard:

> He has the wisdom to keep in front of him the certainty that "they"—the client, market, and public—will always, in the long run, accept his design criteria. His early statement of "being able to make a living doing things I want to do, in the way I want them done" has bolstered many. He accepts market reality as a climber accepts risk: it is always there, not to be disregarded but not the primary condition of the ascent.

Girard drew on his astute knowledge of woodworking, drawing, painting, collage, graphic design, and architecture when approaching the task of designing. He had a deep commitment to experimentation and a lack of fear when it came to following an idea as far as it could go. This kind of approach led to a lifetime of creating unique items that were sometimes highly functional and at others purely aesthetic, both of which Girard revered.

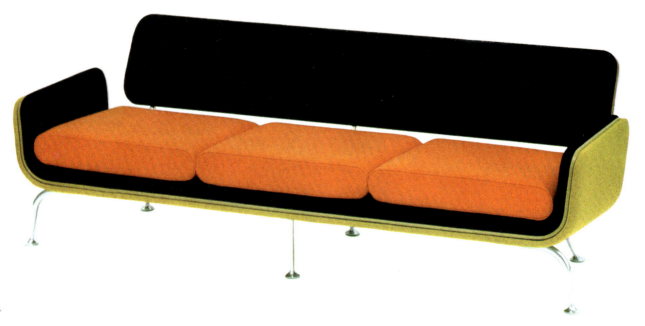

The Girard Group, 1967. Top: Single chair in green with royal blue cushion. Middle: Dot ottoman in magenta and cocoa. Bottom: Three-seater sofa in black, orange, and mustard.

The Girard Group, 1967. Top: Scoop-side ottoman in cream and caramel vinyl with black-and-cream-checked cushion. Middle: Scoop-side chair in neutral combination. Bottom: Tufted, square ottoman in black, cocoa, and mustard.

The Girard Group, 1967. Top: Toast-colored vinyl ottoman with extruded legs. Middle: Scoop-back chair on castors. Bottom: Scoop-armed three-seater sofa in celadon, bark, gray, and cream.

Promotional photos for the Girard Group, 1967.

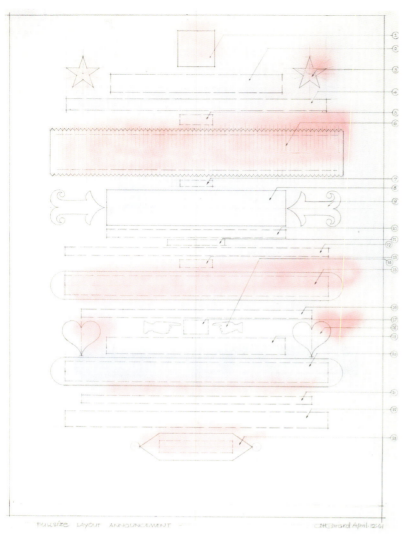

← Top, left: Spacing blueprint for the poster announcing the opening of the Herman Miller Textiles & Objects shop, 1961. Top, right: Marker drawing of the poster announcing the opening of the Textiles & Objects shop, 1961. Bottom, left: Painting for a Textiles & Objects sale poster, gouache on paper, 1961. Bottom, right: Final print of a Textiles & Objects sale poster, 1961.

→ Poster announcing the opening of the Herman Miller Textiles & Objects shop, produced on hand-printed paper, 1961.

In 1961 Alexander Girard broke the textile industry rule that kept showrooms available only to tradespeople. Girard wanted designers to see his latest textiles for Herman Miller, but he didn't know why the public had to be excluded. Herman Miller agreed and opened its showroom to all. The now famous Textiles & Objects (T&O) store was born. At T&O, members of the public could, for the first time, purchase everything on display without going through an interior designer. What they saw was not only a collection of textiles but an environment—a vision pulled directly from Girard's active mind. He designed the showroom from top to bottom, from poster graphics to furnishings, from small objects to large display innovations.

This experimental space was located in a storefront on East 53rd Street in Manhattan. It was a long and narrow space, which Girard painted glossy white. He added white cabinet hardware on white cabinets he designed, a white reception desk, white lampshades, and white shelving of his making (with lights embedded to create a shadowless atmosphere much like a museum). Girard even painted his own exit sign for the back of the shop and designed custom light bulbs that he installed on the ceiling without shades—350 of them set into a grid. He placed some of his own furniture designs in the showroom—chairs, stools, and side tables—and upholstered these pieces with his textiles. He dotted the space with graphic pillows also created from his own designs.

The main attractions were the large swaths of draped fabrics—ninety-four of them—displayed in ingenious configurations. At T&O, Girard magically made each fabric visible and ingestible, despite being near so many others. He hung some textiles on rods, let others hug walls, and draped more over triangular horses. A few textiles sat folded on surfaces, nestled together in intricate folds (showing their available colorways). Girard wasn't satisfied; he also made neckties out of his fabrics and crafted small mirrors that combined small bits of his textiles held in place with pretty brass discs typically used on roof shingles.

At T&O Girard's newest textile designs were exhibited alongside a few Herman Miller classics, and in an unusual move, Girard added non-textile objects from outside makers to the space. These, he felt, would lend ambience and interest. They did, but how he convinced Herman Miller to allow the diffusion of its brand is a mystery—

← Susan Girard pauses on her husband's multicolored tricorn-shaped settee in the Textiles & Objects shop, 1961.

→ Poster for the Textiles & Objects shop using Girard's photograph of his folk art collection from all over the world, 1961.

← Interior of the Textiles & Objects shop, featuring Girard's revolutionary illuminated *étagères* filled with folk art, 1961. Photograph by Charles Eames.

→ Top: Artist Marilyn Neuhart's commissioned dolls made from Girard's textiles, 1961. Bottom: Interior of the Textiles & Objects shop, featuring Girard's tricorn-shaped settee in peacock, fuchsia, and marigold, 1961. Photographs by Charles Eames.

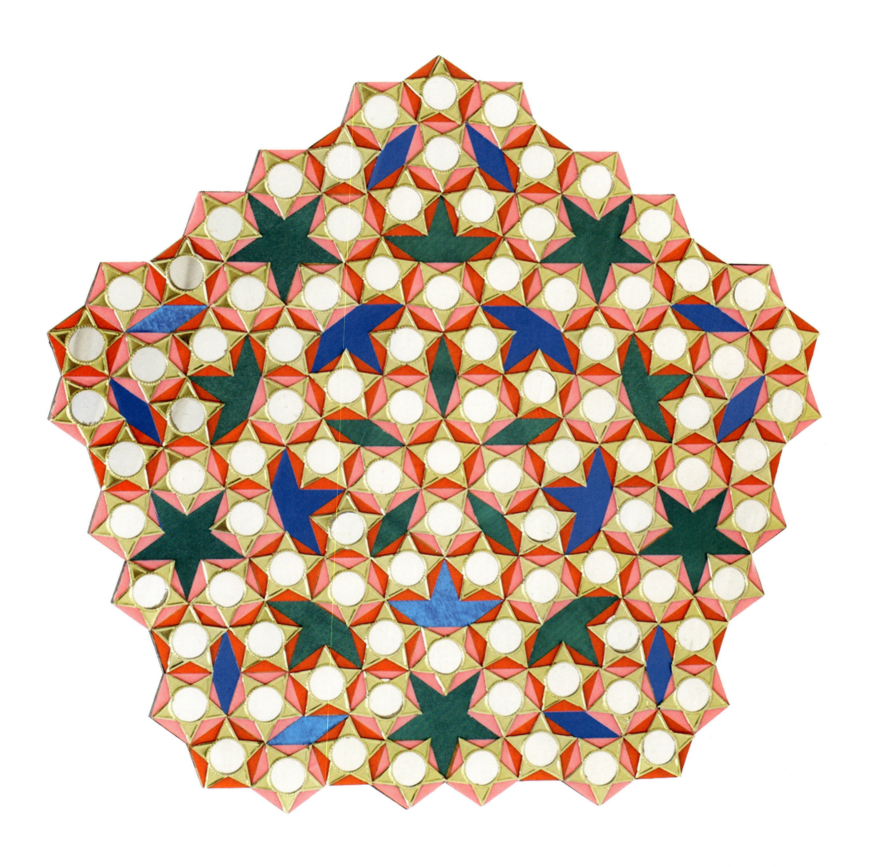

Polygon-shaped mirror made from hand-printed paper collage and small round mirrors for the Textiles & Objects shop, 1961.

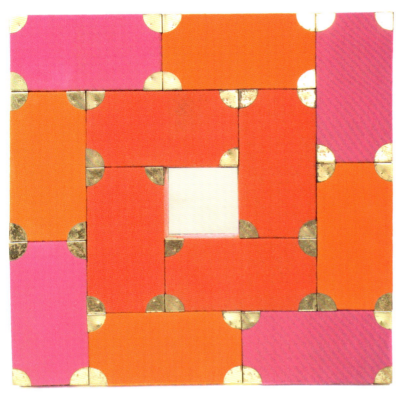
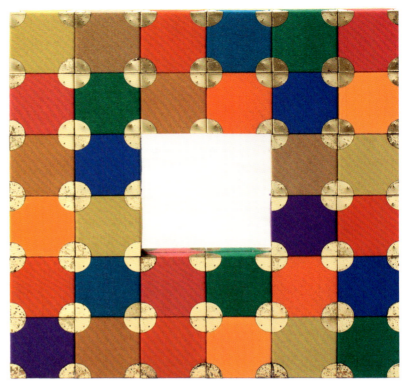

Square mirrors framed in assorted Girard textiles with metal trim normally used to secure shingles to a roof, 1961.

Pillow slipcovers made for the Textiles & Objects shop, 1961.

120 PRODUCT DESIGN

Girard had a special gift for persuading clients and employers to support him in exploring ideas that challenged the status quo and fit the task at hand. The T&O space was chic, lively, and colorful. Every item looked handsome against the white surfaces. *Industrial Design* magazine wrote, "The shop is called, appropriately, Textiles & Objects, and it is a riotous profusion of colors and forms. But for all that, it is meticulously conceived. Everything from its lighting to its cupboard hardware intensifies the general and particular character of the merchandise."

Among the non-Herman Miller objects Girard included in his T&O design were numerous folk art pieces. He had long had a deep love of artisanal work and often took the time to meet and know the artisans themselves. Not only did he see the value and importance of keeping handmade arts and crafts alive, but he believed that by placing them in this new context, they would reach a wider audience. Girard countered the two-dimensional Herman Miller textiles with countless handmade sculptures, clay churches, animal figurines, and even a tiny wooden Ferris wheel. He commissioned fabric dolls to be made for the space by designer Marilyn Neuhart (see page 117). Viewers were encouraged to look at folk art with new eyes.

The *New York Herald Tribune* wrote, "Behind [Girard's] soft-spoken, unassuming manner is a talent for not only finding things but doing amazing things with things." It was said that many Herman Miller employees spent their entire paychecks at T&O.

Typical of his multidisciplinary approach to every undertaking, Girard created a stunning invitation and announcement poster for the T&O opening (see pages 112–13). In the poster he called the objects in the shop "unusual and sympathetic." The poster itself was of unusual and sympathetic design. It was very quickly admired and deemed an exciting graphic work that succeeded by not following the rules (and it is still revered today). Girard's poster fearlessly, joyfully combined eleven different typefaces even though standard guidelines advised designers to use just one. Girard uncommonly placed serifs close to sans serifs and added italics to the mix. Some of his typefaces were elegant and modern, others were squat or strangely kerned (one was incongruously Gothic). The poster was printed on a toothy paper that lent a humble feeling. Technically, nothing about the poster should have been attractive, but it was. Not only that, it was mesmerizing.

The Textiles & Objects shop interior, 1961. Photograph by Charles Eames.

Girard at the opening of the Textiles & Objects shop, 1961.

Girard centered his design classically on the paper. He gave it rich, traditional colors. Then he performed weird tricks around it. He accentuated the address of the store with two curvy arrows pointing to it, and then curiously also emphasized a lone ampersand. The words *Textiles* and *Objects* were constructed out of two typefaces, the lowercase "t" without a full horizontal line across it, while the capital letters were extra brawny and allowed Girard to make a perfectly circular "O," which he favored. The name of the shop sat in a blue rectangle scalloped only on its top and bottom. Other bold silhouettes included a plain rectangle, two lozenge shapes, and a funny circus-like flourish at the bottom. The idiosyncrasies on the poster could easily have looked chaotic, but like the entirety of T&O, in Girard's hands the design felt inspired.

In 1952, the same year Alexander Girard introduced his first textile line with Herman Miller, he also debuted a new collection of wallpapers for his employer. The offering included a range of geometric patterns, some dense and others more sparse. He created elegant typeface designs, stripes, dots, and more. His wallpaper debut had eight introductory designs, each with a choice of five color options for the forefront design and five for the background. Girard wanted to give designers as much versatility as he could.

While Girard had created a number of unique paper wall murals for different projects, when it came to a commercially available collection, he sought to make the offering both versatile and universal. He said, "Wallpaper should be one of two things. Either it should be a mural or it should be merely a textured background on which to hang pictures and decorative objects." With little exception, he held to that and kept representative images out of his collection. A few of his textile patterns were also printed as wallpapers, but more often his wallpaper designs were unique to themselves. His patterns sat chicly on walls and complemented many different design schemes. The *New York Herald Tribune* wrote, "Mr. Girard believes wallpaper should produce a feeling of texture, of 'change of pace' on a wall without being obvious."

As was his custom, Girard also orchestrated all the details of how the collection was presented and marketed. The cover of the sample book was relatively spare and featured his signature from the 1930s—a triangle for "A," a square for "H," and a circle for "G"—as shapes upon which he laid the other titular type. This composition was a nod to the graphic design of the Bauhaus, which Girard greatly admired. Girard's original ad campaign was a series of photos taken by Charles Eames using minimal environments

← Left: Girard-designed spiral wallpaper pattern books, 1952. Right: Traditional wallpaper sample book, 1952.

↑ Colorways of *Alphabet*, single-color print, 1951.

← Colorways of *Pepitas*, single-color print, 1952.

→ Colorways of *Retrospective*, single-color print, 1952.

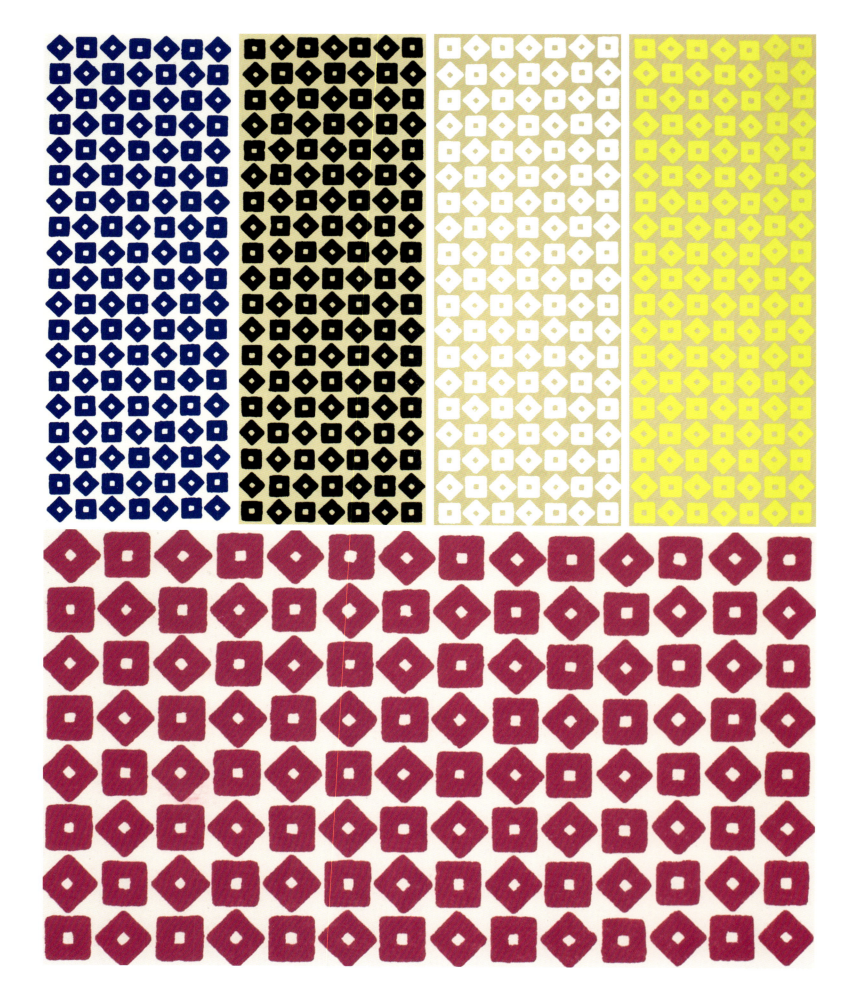

which featured the wallpapers with folk art and furniture from Herman Miller. This kind of pairing, while old hat for Girard, was still quite new and unusual for the time.

Girard once said, "In general I can say I have accepted jobs where a new prototype may be developed … For my own satisfaction, I have taken jobs which allow me as much variety as possible." This was true of his wallpaper collection, which Herman Miller produced for twelve years. Just as Girard's textiles changed the look of many interior designs, his wallpapers also transformed environments in clever ways, lending them an air of modern refinement.

In 1971 Alexander Girard was called upon once again to bring his mastery of graphic design and color to a new project. The designer Robert Propst had been working with Herman Miller to reinvent office environments through a design concept called Action Office, which embodied modern office furniture in extremely restrained environments. It featured one of the first examples (if not the first) of an office cubicle. Girard's artful innovation arrived in the form of forty silkscreened panels featuring a wide range of single graphic images. Propst's designs were monochromatic and spare, and they benefitted greatly from Girard's whimsical line of colorful silkscreens, which Herman Miller named Environmental Enrichment Panels. Girard's panels did exactly that: they enriched and enlivened Action Office workspaces. Over five years, Girard's beautifully large silkscreens were installed on Action Office walls and ceilings. The panels were a transformational addition to Propst's vision and a rare instance when Girard contributed to an environment without designing it altogether.

Girard's silkscreens brought warmth and color, lent vital notes of handcrafted artistry, and breathed life into Propst's office designs. The scale of the silkscreens was stirring. Each of them held one sizable, nonrepeating image. Girard thought of these panels as hanging murals as opposed to draped curtains. As such, each silkscreen came in one prescribed size only; they were never sold by the yard or in custom dimensions. Girard first developed his concept for each

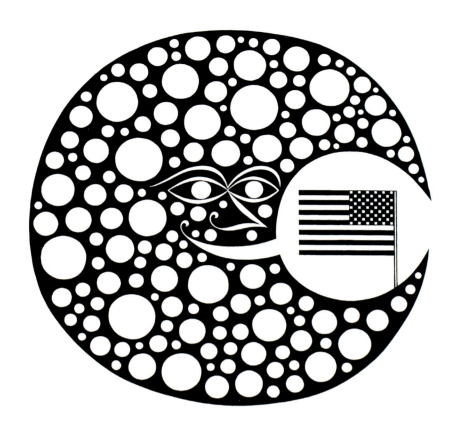

P. 128 Colorways of *Square Diamonds*, single-color print, 1952.

P. 129 Colorways of *Dots*, single-color print, 1951.

P. 130 Colorways of *Dashes*, five-color print, 1951.

P. 131 Colorways of *Broken Stripe*, five-color print, 1951.

← Girard surrounded by original drawings from his Environmental Enrichment Panels collection for Herman Miller, 1971.

→ Top: *Moon*, single-color print on *Mexicotton* basecloth, 47" × 47", 1972. Bottom: Announcement of Environmental Enrichment Panels collection, 1972.

design as a small sketch, then later as a gigantic, full-scale drawing. In their final placements, Girard's panels stretched along office walls, surprised employees from ceilings, and marked many otherwise unremarkable ends of hallways.

His silkscreens included a large number of geometric shapes as well as more figurative images, such as richly colored hearts, suns, snakes, castles, flowers, and people. He created one mesmerizing panel, *Triple Eyes*, which showed different-colored pupils, a funny abbreviated gesture for a nose, a sprig of forehead lines (or eyebrow hair), and a beguiling gaze. This was one of many instances when Girard identified a historic symbol with a tremendously large ancestry and added his voice to the mix. He had observed eye imagery in cultures both ancient and contemporary (eyes had been employed as meaningful symbols in Greece, Egypt, Turkey, and many other countries). Another such symbol with a long design history that Girard used for his Environmental Enrichment Panels was the sun (a symbol he had observed in cultures around the world). Girard was drawn to these types of images that stitched together eras and people.

This collection of Environmental Enrichment Panels can be seen as Girard's lexicon; through it, one can interpret what he felt was both important and universal as a means to "enrich" an environment. As Girard's last project for Herman Miller, it seems to be a distillation of his design career at large, as it includes all the aspects he was most interested in: architecture, color, pattern, nature, and humanity. While the panels were only in production for a short time, this group of graphics has gone on to influence generations of designers and their impact can still be seen today.

← *Stars*, single-color print on *Mexicotton* basecloth, 47" × 65", 1972.

→ *Girls*, seven-color print on *Mexicotton* basecloth, 47" × 65", 1972.

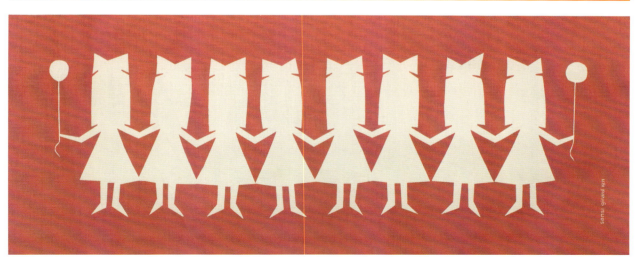

← Top: *New Sun*, single-color print on *Mexicotton* basecloth, 47" × 47", 1972. Middle: *Hand and Dove*, single-color print on *Mexicotton* basecloth, 25" × 50", 1972. Bottom: *Paper Dolls*, single-color print on *Mexicotton* basecloth, 25" × 50", 1972.

P. 141 *Black and White*, single-color print on *Mexicotton* basecloth, 45" × 58", 1972.

Bouquet, single-color print on striped *Mexicotton* basecloth, 47" × 47", 1972. This is the only Environmental Enrichment Panel printed on a patterned basecloth.

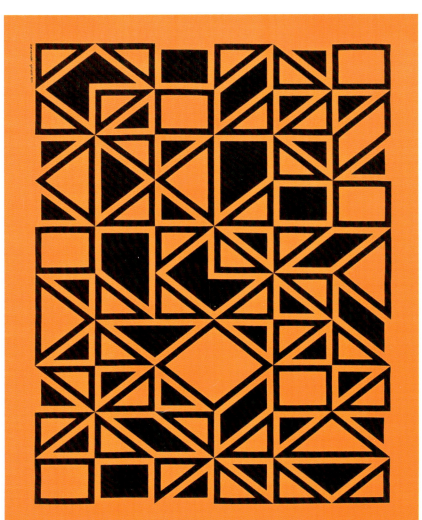

Textile designer Jack Lenor Larsen's words about Girard's work in interior design could be explicitly applied to his silkscreened Environmental Enrichment Panels. Larsen called Girard's designs "often perfectly orchestrated demonstrations of how to use his fabrics effectively." Girard's Environmental Enrichment Panels were modern and stylish. They connected with Propst's not-overly-joyful office concept, and then fully redefined the Action Office tone, and by proxy, office life itself.

In 1955 the Georg Jensen housewares store in Manhattan invited Alexander Girard to reexamine concepts in table settings. As a result, Girard produced two lines of inspired dinnerware for Jensen. One had diverse and saturated colored circles. The other included more white space with varying geometric patterns and facets of gold leaf. Girard's designs were a departure from the norm; they looked fresh and new. The fact that they didn't appear in sets of identical pieces was a bit of a revolution. Girard liked variety, so although each set had a clear commonality, the pieces were built to be arranged and rearranged by each customer. If a host wanted to place a plum-colored bowl on a turquoise plate, Girard's tableware encouraged this. If they wanted to have a plate with a hexagon sitting next to a plate with a teardrop design, they could do that very easily, too. With each bowl in the dinnerware set that featured dollops of color, Girard placed the bright hues intentionally low where they would be obscured by food. Placed this way, when the bowl was filled, the dinnerware looked simply white; only while eating or drinking would its color be pleasantly revealed.

In 1956, a year after Girard's dinnerware came out, Georg Jensen asked him to style eight unique table settings for a promotional event in its store. Once again, Girard swiftly strayed from the ordinary. He placed antique and new items together on each table. He used items culled from the Georg Jensen store, from flea markets, and from his own cupboards. His mixture of diverse dinnerware was not what hosts were generally practicing, but in Girard's hands, the result was inspiring. It gave people permission to be inventive, to have fun, and to create a tablescape that reflected their own style and taste. Jack Lenor Larsen wrote about Girard's contribution to Georg Jensen, "The history-making demonstration heralded a whole new attitude toward the sensual and social pleasures of dining ... Sandro Girard's underlying proposition was becoming clearer: he was urging us to celebrate, not stifle with intellectualized precepts, areas that innately belong to the senses."

Girard created eight dramatically different tables for Georg Jensen's promotional event. He designed his own line of place mats for the occasion and added these to one table scheme. Because he would not be producing them himself, he supplied Georg Jensen with exacting blueprints. Girard included many nonessential props on his styled tables. Some had nothing to do with dining but lent a mood: a deck of playing cards, a cabinet artistically covered in sardine tins, a wrapped gift, his own castlelike sculpture. Girard included name cards on the tables that he had made from corks and construction paper (humble materials for a high-end housewares company). All of the cards were gracefully hand-lettered by Girard. He could barely stop playing with this bit of theater and wrote long descriptions of what type of person each table suited. His profile of one table's guests read as follows (the lack of capital letters is Girard's):

> A FAMILY—mother, father and two children— has just come in from a morning of sailing. they are about to have a hearty bowl of soup, good bread, cold cuts, and cheeses. this family thoroughly enjoys being together and has fun living. the teenage daughter likes to surprise with fanciful table decorations and for the occasion has made one of chinese papers. the accessories—plates, dishes, and bowls—were bought on family trips. though very different in character, the elements of the table setting, used as they are in happy relationship of good friends, blend harmoniously, reflecting the togetherness of the family.

Girard designed a very beautiful announcement for his Georg Jensen event. He set his custom curling typeface onto stiff paper that he cut into the silhouette of a molded dessert. In the 5th Avenue Georg Jensen display window, rather than promote his own dinnerware or place mats, Girard playfully set out miniatures of each of his table settings, replete with tiny servings of faux food. He was much more fond of delivering delight than he was of announcing his own accomplishments.

P. 142 Announcement for the Girard for Georg Jensen collection that hung in the windows of the Georg Jensen Store in New York City, acrylic on 1" plywood, approximately 30" tall, 1956.

P. 143 Left: Girard for Georg Jensen collection of porcelain coffee cups with colored interiors, 1956. Right: Soup bowls from the same collection that are colored to just below the fill line so the colors reveal themselves while being eaten from.

P. 144–145 Eight plate designs from the Girard for Georg Jensen collection, some of which feature metallic gold leaf, 1956.

↑ Girard for Georg Jensen collection, 1956. Left: Alexander and Susan styling the tabletops for the collection's opening. Right: Tabletop design.

→ Girard for Georg Jensen collection, 1956. Top: Tabletop design for the collection, featuring a cabinet face made from sardine tins. Bottom: Tabletop design.

Braniff International Airways

BEFORE 1965 BRANIFF INTERNATIONAL
Airways was a smallish, unremarkable airline with sixty-five planes that traveled mostly from the Southwest and Midwest United States to global locations. When Braniff expanded its destinations in South America, it desired a new look to accompany its growth. Braniff approached the New York ad agency Jack Tinker & Partners to lead the brand change, and agency executive Mary Wells hired Alexander Girard. While Wells wrote many clever advertisements for Braniff, Girard was asked to redesign Braniff's visual identity. He jumped in without reserve, making literally more than one thousand changes to airport spaces, airplanes, and signage. He avoided anodyne corporate tendencies and imparted on Braniff a daring sense of color infused with unique textures and style. The industry took notice. By the end of the collaboration, Girard had offered up a wholly new experience in air travel.

    One influential change Girard made was to create a custom typeface for Braniff and streamline its logo, making it stylish and modern. He added a rotating crop of colorways and created an enthusiastic number of variations to his logo by abbreviating it, tilting its letters, dividing and rearranging them, working them into endless configurations. These landed on Braniff's airport signage, plane tickets, luggage tags, stationery, playing cards, matchbooks, and more. His graphics for Braniff became quickly recognizable and admired.

Girard then brought his expertise from more than a decade at the helm of Herman Miller's textile division to Braniff's airplane seats and lounges and created fifty-six custom textiles. These were new iterations of his famously vivid striped, checked, and solid textiles. He also created one futuristic black-and-white textile composed of his newly drafted Braniff typeface. Girard layered textiles joyfully on plane seats, used them as section dividers, and draped them on airport lounge windows.

Girard had worked on a number of commercial spaces in the past. Despite this, he drenched Braniff in *non*commercial ideas, beginning with the interior design of its lounges. Girard's furniture in Braniff's airport lounges—also upholstered in his textiles—included his own custom-designed sofas and chairs with slender legs, all more delicate than most airport furniture. He added his own custom stools and commissioned rows of red fiberglass chairs designed by his friend Charles Eames. Antithetical to what most airports were doing at the time, the only furniture bolted to the floor were the Eames chairs. Girard placed area rugs in the Braniff lounges rather than industrial-grade carpet. He hung travel posters on the walls and stocked shelves with charming folk art from South America—some of which was from his personal collection. The effect of Girard's changes taken altogether was inviting, lively. *Progressive Architecture* wrote, "The major contribution of this corporate image design, then, is not its decorative effect, but a broader dimension—the psychological benefits to the individual traveler that masterly decoration can unexpectedly provide." Girard, having long been an avid traveler himself, was humanizing air travel.

While many designers would have crafted a company rebrand by performing only the changes requested by their client, Girard never paused to consider this. As he set his mind to the interiors of the planes, he left nothing unchanged. He installed his custom textiles on airplane seats in color families that stayed intact but might alternately be in checked, striped, or solid incarnations. This gave seat rows unity in tone while avoiding predictability. In typical fashion, he also lent his vision to the smallest of details, emblazoning his graphics on everything from sugar, salt, and pepper packets to menus, bathroom soaps, luggage tags, matchbooks, cocktail napkins, and even new airsick bags. Girard even reimagined the way the employees inside the planes looked, selecting Emilio Pucci to create vivid pilot and flight attendant uniforms that were unlike anything in the industry.

Girard eagerly addressed Braniff's plane exteriors as well. He chose seven colors and doused the jets in solid swaths of them. Girard said, "The idea was to make the plane like a great racing car—with the fuselage painted a solid color clearly expressing its shape." The fleet looked not only colorful but noticeably rid of the usual stripes and complex graphics of most airplanes. *Mechanics* magazine

152 BRANIFF INTERNATIONAL AIRWAYS

dubbed Braniff's orange Boeing 727 the Super Carrot. Girard was undoubtedly amused. He painted all the equipment surrounding the planes with the same vivid hues—things such as moving stairways, ladders, luggage wagons, and gas trucks. Girard was extending his magic out as far as it could go.

Girard's designs were embraced and employed to Braniff's advantage. Mary Wells initiated an ad campaign that called this "the end of the plain plane." She filmed a TV ad featuring Andy Warhol sitting next to Sonny Liston on a Braniff plane, and Whitey Ford next to Salvador Dalí. The copy read, "When you got it—flaunt it." *Business Week* wrote, "After years of semi-stagnation, Braniff, by embracing color as a way of life and revving up its overall operations, has become not only the most talked about airline in the world but one of the fastest growing ones as well."

Even without a traveler clocking every Girard flourish, the overall impression of his Braniff redesign was profound. He moved the brand from standardized to highly individual, and no one had ever seen anything like it.

P. 148–149 Braniff fabric designs produced by Herman Miller, 1965.

P. 150 Top: Orange-and-red-checked ottoman with extruded metal legs. Middle: Scoop armchair in mustard with red-and-berry-striped cushion. Bottom: Loveseat in forest green with beige welting and a Granny Smith apple green-and-teal-striped cushion, 1965.

P. 151 Promotional photo of Braniff plane interiors, 1965.

← Top: Check-in desk at a Braniff airport terminal, 1965. Bottom: Waiting lounge interior, 1965, with curtains featuring Girard's futuristic logo textile. The red chairs were designed by Charles Eames.

→ In-plane posters of folk art from Latin America, 1965.

BRANIFF INTERNATIONAL

BRANIFF INTERNATIONAL

alexander girard '65

P. 154 Braniff promotional poster, 1965.

P. 155 Promotional photo from Braniff, 1965.

← Braniff flight attendant boots designed by Emilio Pucci on Girard's furniture covered in the orange-and-red colorway of Checkers, 1965.

P. 161–162 Braniff promotional posters, 1965.

P. 163 Promotional photo of a Braniff boarding lounge, 1965.

P. 164 Promotional photo of one of Braniff's airport lounges, 1965.

P. 165 Braniff promotional poster, 1965.

BRANIFF INTERNATIONAL
BRANIFF INTERNATIONAL
BRANIFF INTERNATIONAL
BRANIFF INTERNATIONAL
BRANIFF INTERNATIONAL
BRANIFF INTERNATIONAL
BRANIFF INTERNATIONAL
BRANIFF INTERNATIONAL
BRANIFF INTERNATIONAL
BRANIFF INTERNATIONAL

BRANIFF AIRWAYS, INCORPORATED · ANNUAL REPORT · 1965

BI BI BI
BRANIFF INTERNATIONAL

BI BI BI
BRANIFF INTERNATIONAL

BI BI BI
BRANIFF INTERNATIONAL

BI BI BI
BRANIFF INTERNATIONAL

BI BI BI
BRANIFF INTERNATIONAL

BI BI BI

alexander girard 65

A small selection from the dozens of objects and graphic designs that Girard made for Braniff International Airways, 1965.

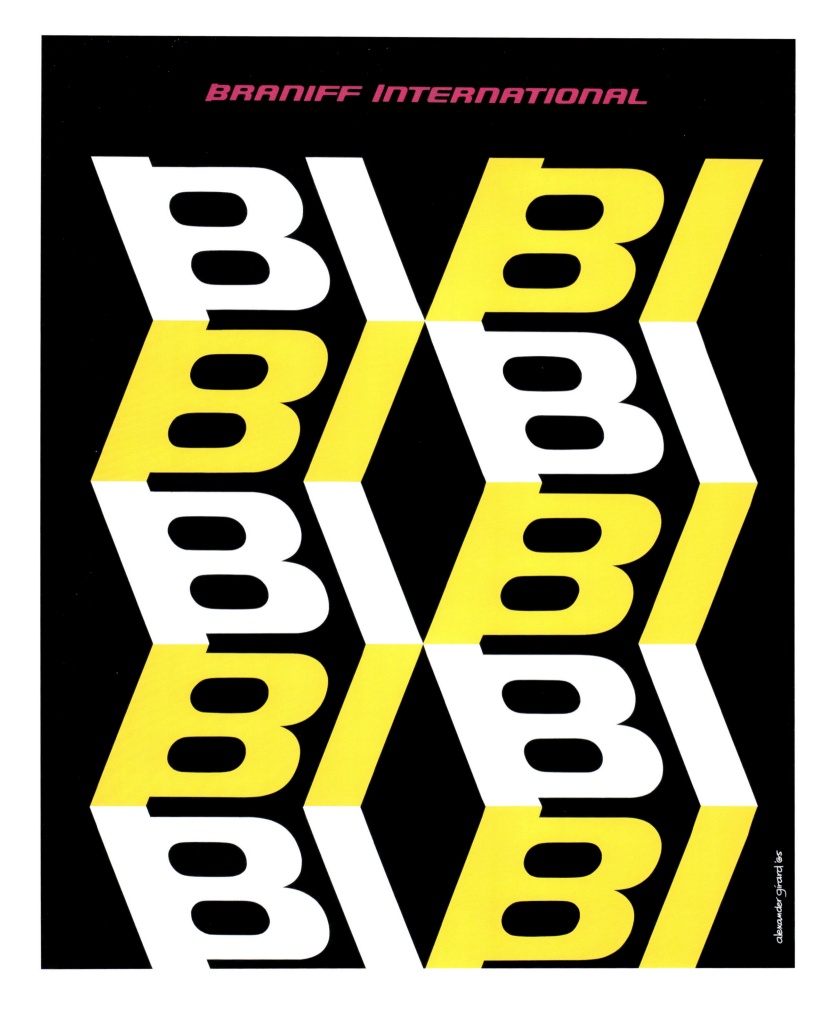

Detrola

IN 1943 ALEXANDER GIRARD—THEN A freelance architect and interior, product, and graphic designer—was hired as chief designer for the Detrola Corporation, a Detroit communications company. Girard was brought on to design radios and record players, and when he arrived, another designer was already at Detrola—the now-famous Charles Eames. The two quickly saw how much their aesthetics overlapped. After seeing some radio sketches Girard had left out on his desk, Eames wrote to him: "I see you already have all of this, so you don't need me." The two became lifelong friends and colleagues. They went on to collaborate on a number of varied projects, from exhibitions and films to their overlapping careers at Herman Miller. The friendship came to include their wives and families, and the couples traveled and spent holidays together on several occasions. Girard later said of Eames, "I don't know anyone else who has gotten into the problem of design in such a profound way, really, and without ignoring all the historical aspects."

P. 166–167 Girard designed radios and turntables that sometimes resembled his wife Susan's elegant handbags, 1940s.

← Top: Detrola bent-wood radio with wooden knobs, 1940s. Bottom: Detrola blonde bent-wood radio, 1940s.

→ Girard redesigned the cafeteria at Detrola with sinewy walls and soaring ceilings, 1940s.

While Girard the product designer was hired by Detrola, soon his other skills crowded the workroom. Without being asked, he gleefully overstepped his job description. He worked on product designs as expected, but also redesigned everything in his office: he created slanted display shelves to set his drawings on, he buried flat files in the wall so their drawers lay flush with the surface, and he designed a uniquely oval desk for himself, with a pop-up drafting board on its surface. He also set his attention to small details, such as cabinet pulls that were modern and chic ovoid cutouts. When the Detrola executives saw Girard's office, they asked him to redesign their spaces as well, which he did happily.

Girard soon transformed Detrola's conference rooms too, outfitting them with uniquely scalloped tables and built-in sofas upholstered in saturated colors. The rest of Detrola's common spaces did not escape his attention for long: secretaries soon worked at new versions of Girard's sinuous desk and sat beside unusual shelves he devised for their papers. At some point Girard came to eat at Detrola's unstylish company cafeteria. Before long he seductively wrapped its columns in curved, purple-stained plywood and laid linoleum on the floor in colored stripes. In 1945 *Institutions* magazine wrote, "The two-year-old cafeteria in the plant of Detrola Corporation, Detroit, represents a triumph of design and engineering over handicaps in the structure where it is housed. As a matter of fact, the limitations of the building were turned, insofar as possible, into advantages." Girard was full of innovation and solved problems where he saw them—for example, he designed a two-sided clock that was cleverly readable from either direction down the hallway.

Girard's extensive redesign of Detrola was the first glimpse anyone had been given of his omnivorous vision—his ability to focus on everything at the same time. Later in his career he would be hired specifically for this attribute, but at Detrola it came as a surprise. In the course of his stay there, Girard came to reimagine even the factory space itself. He improved the utility and aesthetics of the factory area, creating better lighting and new surfaces. He once again applied his curved ovoid themes, but here in economical materials such as pine and rubber. By the time he left Detrola, Girard had lent his attention to so many areas, there was barely an inch that didn't reflect his vision. While he had outperformed client goals on many previous projects, the visibility of his work for Detrola broadcast Girard's skills to a larger audience than before.

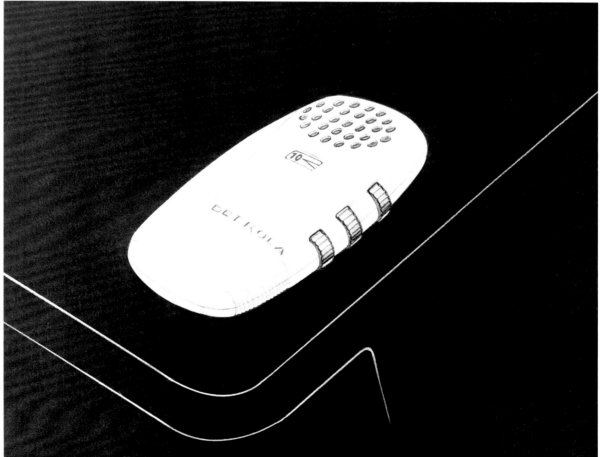

← Spare turntable design for Detrola, 1940s.

→ Portable radio designs for Detrola, 1940s.

← Top: Reception area at Detrola, 1940s. Bottom: Executive dining room with fuchsia chairs and a red reverse-scalloped dining table, 1940s.

→ Top: Executive office at Detrola with ovoid desk, 1940s. Bottom: Executive office at Detrola with built-in shelves, 1940s.

173

← Top: Girard in his office, featuring an adjustable drafting table and display picture rails, 1940s. Bottom: Reception area with unique *Out* and *In* shelves, 1940s.

→ Girard redesigned the Detrola factory lines into elegant efficiency, 1940s.

Curation and Exhibition Design

BEGINNING IN THE 1940S, ALEXANDER Girard's work included curation and exhibition design. The practice of curation was something Girard had been exploring from the time he was a young man—first in his family's antique furniture business and then in the design and execution of his first apartment. While Girard could, and often did, design all aspects of a project, he was also capable and interested in curating the work of others. More than the value of any one idea, object, or project, Girard saw the value in the visual collage. Creating relationships and conversations within his curation often led the viewer to come to a new or deeper understanding of the work. The exhibitions were undeniably alluring no matter their topic: textiles, modern furnishings, John Deere. Girard's exhibition work was a clear manifestation of his thorough understanding of architecture and how a space is experienced from the exterior and throughout. He led spectators thoughtfully through each space using well-timed pauses, subtle directional changes, and widely varied lighting schemes. To allow contemplation, he positioned areas that were flooded with information near others with sparser arrangements. Time and again, Girard orchestrated highly communicative journeys through each showroom, museum exhibition, or gallery display.

In 1937 Girard moved from New York to Michigan, where he and his wife, Susan, bought a home and started a family. During the next two decades—a time when many types of design moved into new, modern expressions—Girard envisioned and curated a number of influential exhibitions that focused on contemporary furnishings and objects. These were part of a nascent conversation the design world was having about the value and definition of *modern*.

Contemporary, clean-lined furnishings were moving away from older, heftier silhouettes. Girard and his peers were slimming designs down, inventing furniture that thoughtfully interacted with human bodies (ergonomic chairs) and creating storage that showed its bones (open shelving with visible hardware). It was an exciting time in design, and many of the shows Girard designed had lofty names that reflected this, such as *Good Design*, *An Exhibition for Modern Living*, *Space for an Open Mind*, and *Everyday Art Gallery*. For all its optimism, the modern furnishings movement also met with some resistance. There were unconvinced citizens who felt the new interiors were extreme and too spare. Girard, being preternaturally skilled at making extraordinary ideas seem natural, was an ideal curator for these exhibitions.

In 1946 Girard designed the *Everyday Art Gallery* exhibitions at the Walker Art Center in Minneapolis. He curated and designed *An Exhibition for Modern Living* at the Detroit Institute of Arts in 1949, a room in *Space for an Open Mind* at the Grand Rapids Furniture Museum in 1951, and the *Good Design* show at the Chicago Merchandise Mart in 1953 and the Museum of Modern Art, New York, in 1954. During his own explorations of what *modern* really meant, Girard wrote, "*Modern* then is an adjective that is synonymous with new, or young; and as everything, including ourselves, are new, or young and modern at least once—then everything is at one time modern. In terms of design, an object can only be modern when it is the most recent expression of a solution to a problem. As soon as a better answer is found, the design and object ceases to be modern and belongs to the past." Girard assured visitors of the merit of modern design by displaying furniture that was simple and highly adaptive to a multitude of environments. In one of his exhibitions, he installed slanted walls with partial roofs that looked like charming stage sets. In another he built a textured wall of rustic wood and covered it with splendid modern graphics (bridging the old and the new). He found ways to make modern furnishings palatable to many.

Girard's shows were persuasive, inclusive. He placed furnishings in settings people could walk into and investigate. His task for each exhibition was twofold: to promote new design ideas—which he adamantly believed in—and to create a pleasing display. He sometimes accentuated furniture pieces with a few playful folk art sculptures or an occasional live plant. This was his way of adding hints of a welcoming (not overly severe) home.

Hilde Reiss, curator at the Walker Art Center (including of *Everyday Art Gallery*), made the point that this kind of forward motion in design was necessary. He wrote:

Let's look critically at the objects around us ... Are our utensils, our furniture as satisfactory as they could be? Are they designed for the needs of today? Or are they sentimental hangovers from the past? Do our lighting fixtures pretend to be dripping candles or kerosene lamps; or are they clean, simple forms honestly expressive of the age of electricity? Are our chairs designed for great-grandmother's hoopskirts and whalebone corsets, or do they fit the natural contours of the comfortably clothed figure of today?

A reviewer of the Walker Art Center show wrote of Girard's design, "The informality, freedom from clutter, excellent lighting, and general attractiveness of the display frees the spectator from the usual museum fatigue."

In the planning stages for any exhibition he curated, Girard chose pieces very carefully, selecting items that perfectly (and collectively) exemplified modern design. While mapping out the show *An Exhibition for Modern Living*, he took more than a year to assemble the right combination of sofas, chairs, shelves, lamps, and rugs. Girard then drafted eye-catching ways to display them.

The last of Girard's exhibition designs that focused predominantly on modern furnishings was at the 1954 *Good Design* show at the Museum of Modern Art (MoMA) in New York City. Here the crowd had already accepted modern design's value, and Girard went to town; he created more extravagant schemes than he had elsewhere. He delineated an area of the MoMA show with a large paper curtain that had diamond-shaped cutouts. Through the cutouts a visitor could see Girard's sweeping wall of textiles. Above these hung a mass of geometrically folded papers on the ceiling like a chic set of prismatic clouds. In other areas of that show Girard minimized backgrounds dramatically in order to highlight his selected home furnishings. He painted those walls and ceilings black, covered nearby floors with black vinyl-impregnated cork, and placed dark flocked paper on the inner partitions of shelves. Then he lit the objects from nearly invisible sources. *Retailing Daily* wrote, "Sources of light are not discernible, so that the merchandise on display stands out in sharp relief." The *New York Herald Tribune* wrote, "Dramatically highlighted ... each item was ringed by a beam of bright light and set against a velvet black background to give a floating appearance ... One is not

conscious of the source of light; it seems to come from nowhere and envelops the individual exhibits."

In 1961 Girard returned to exhibition design with a Nativity-themed folk art show that he curated and designed at the Museum of International Folk Art in Santa Fe, New Mexico. Starting with this exhibition, Girard revealed a new style. His designs were ultimately meant to highlight the work of the folk artists, letting their vision and hand take center stage. Girard was not trying to convince anyone to embrace his definition of modern but instead focused on the celebration of the objects being displayed. His exhibitions still had his fingerprints all over them and included superb lighting, unusual graphics, and a profound understanding of pace, but the shows became abundant, elaborate, and fun. From 1961 to 1981, Girard arranged mesmerizing swarms of objects into wondrously detailed displays. These included folk art shows in two cities titled *The Nativity* (1961 and 1962), a large work for John Deere motor company (1964), a display at the World's Fair in San Antonio (1968), and a permanent exhibition at the Museum of International Folk Art (1981). In these curatorial designs, Girard artfully piled preposterous numbers of things together. This excited him and excited viewers. The most modest of his folk art exhibitions were his Nativity shows, each displaying 2,209 folk art figures. He said of his interest in Nativity crafts, which had started when he was a boy, "The collection grew with my maturing and it expanded with my awareness. It was international, it had differences, it was a spectrum of mankind, it was bewilderingly varied and astonishingly related."

In 1964 celebrated architect Eero Saarinen drafted and built a new modern headquarters for the John Deere company in Moline, Illinois. To celebrate the building as well as honor Deere's more than one hundred years of manufacturing farming equipment, Saarinen hired Alexander Girard to create a special artwork in the new building's lobby. Girard created a 180-foot-long, 8-foot-tall installation that spanned the entire length of the lobby and comprised more than two thousand vintage objects that related to John Deere history and general agricultural life (see pages 176–78). As was his custom when telling a visual story through objects, he encased the whole collage in a perfectly lit glass vitrine.

Girard and his wife, Susan, went on frequent buying trips around the Midwest for more than a year to gather the items for the Deere artwork. This was fun for the Girards, the kind of treasure hunt they adored—one not hampered by too many strict categories. In addition to visiting flea markets, he politely plundered the offices of the John Deere staff, asking them to lend him special items from their offices. John A. Kouwenhoven, a professor at Barnard College and former editor at *Harper's* magazine, wrote:

Even private offices of the company's executives were stripped of fondly treasured items. I remember the good-natured resignation with which one factory manager parted with an old photograph that the director of public relations spotted on his wall when we stopped in to talk with him one day ... The manager wondered if a copy of the photograph couldn't be sent to Santa Fe so he could keep the original. I don't know whether or not a copy was made, but if it was, it is in his office. The original is incorporated in Girard's design.

After selecting the items for the John Deere project, Girard began orchestrating it back in his Santa Fe studio. He meticulously created a scale replica of the mural in which one square inch equaled one square foot of the John Deere lobby and blank pieces of paper were used to represent each object. This allowed Girard to start manipulating his design. He shuffled these papers for months, remembering what each slip represented (he had an otherworldly recall for objects). In the next phase, Girard's slips of paper were cut into the proper scale and silhouette of each treasure. Kouwenhoven said:

I have been in the drafting room when he has discarded a mere rectangle and with a pair of scissors has cut out as a replacement an accurately scaled miniature silhouette of some complicated form, with no guide but the precise image in his mind's eye. When to the rest of us he seemed to be moving pieces of paper from place to place on that flat white surface, he was actually establishing relationships between real objects in three-dimensional space.

Girard moved on to a larger-scale model of his mural later. There, drawings of each object replaced his paper cutouts. When he finally returned to Moline with every physical item in attendance, he began building. He allowed Saarinen's airy space to inspire changes to his plan and moved items here or there to account for light and balance.

While many elements in the mural related directly to the John Deere company—staff photographs, John Deere advertisements, miniature salesman samples of manure spreaders, and life-sized plow models, for example—Girard also included items that represented home life in Illinois. The *Moline Dispatch* wrote, "The priceless heritage of American agriculture is being immortalized in a sweeping 3-dimensional display." Girard placed common artifacts in this artwork—things such as baskets, spinning wheels, and farm tools. By showcasing items people had routinely interacted with, Girard was inviting viewers to see them as designs for possibly the first time.

P. 176–177 Girard's epic installation at the Eero Saarinen-designed John Deere headquarters in Moline, Illinois, 1964.

P. 178 Girard installing more than one thousand objects for display at the John Deere headquarters in Moline, Illinois, 1964.

P. 179 A tattooed man and a Girard-designed Detrola radio greeted visitors at the Walker Art Center's exhibition entrance of *Everyday Art Gallery* in Minneapolis, Minnesota, 1946.

P. 181 Wood-inlay table with Detrola radio for the Girard-designed exhibition *Everyday Art Gallery* at the Walker Art Center in Minneapolis, Minnesota, 1946.

P. 182 Display cabinet featuring Girard's articulated wooden toys, *Everyday Art Gallery* at the Walker Art Center in Minneapolis, Minnesota, 1946.

P. 183 Girard-designed early plywood furniture and table created for Knoll, *Everyday Art Gallery* at the Walker Art Center in Minneapolis, Minnesota, 1946.

← *An Exhibition for Modern Living*, Detroit Institute of Arts, Detroit, Michigan, 1949. Top: Girard included customizable shelving designed by Eames and various folk art in the exhibition. Bottom: Kitchenware display.

→ *Good Design*, Museum of Modern Art, New York City, 1954. Top: Passageway lined with Girard-designed textile panels on the wall and cutout, layered paper on the ceiling, with chairs by Michael Thonet and Eero Saarinen. Bottom: Paper cutout screens, also designed by Girard, allowed views into other galleries.

EXHIBITION GIRARD COLLECTION MUSEUM OF INTERNATIONAL FOLK ART SANTA FE NEW MEXICO

← Girard designed the typeface for the poster promoting his exhibition *Multiple Visions: A Common Bond* at the Museum of International Folk Art, Santa Fe, New Mexico, 1981.

→ Sketch for the *Multiple Visions: A Common Bond* exhibition poster, paint and marker on brown paper, 1981.

Girard's densely layered mural for John Deere was extraordinarily beautiful even as it was composed of ordinary things. He included gardening tools, muffin tins, quilts, ledger books, personal letters, award ribbons, and buggy wheels. He gave equal weight to election buttons and a weathervane, pitchfork, milking stool, horse collar, clock, apple peeler, and cherry pitter. Girard said, "I did not want to make the mural a chronological list of items or an ethnological or analytical cataloging of them, but rather wanted to give the smell and feel of the period." He backed the entire artwork with weathered boards he had scrupulously gathered from old buildings. The objects overall, arranged in the lush way Girard envisioned them, began to transcend their everyday status. Kouwenhoven wrote, "It seems to me that what Girard has achieved is something unique in modern architecture: a deeply textured, colorful and serenely unified wall, thoroughly in keeping with the subdued elegance of Saarinen's structure. Yet it is alive with fascinating details that are unexpectedly congruous in his witty and luminous juxtapositions. To think of this design as a mural is to diminish what is essentially an architectural achievement."

The mural Girard created was a draw for John Deere employees and the larger Moline community, who came to see what Girard had done with this massive collection of seemingly ordinary objects. Viewers pored over the installation for long periods of time, finding many points of reference. Most had not realized how expressively their design history would stack up. Girard, as an outsider, had managed to remind them of how special their local heritage was. Many years later, John Deere fully restored the mural to preserve it for generations to come.

Following his John Deere project, Girard curated and designed several colorful, intricate shows using his impressive folk art collection (he was an avid collector by then). His pavilion at the 1968 World's Fair in San Antonio, Texas, was full of dense arrangements of folk art, each holding more detail than any viewer could possibly digest at once. Girard underplayed this excess and said modestly, "I've tried to do everything possible to introduce variety, so the scenes will never become all the same."

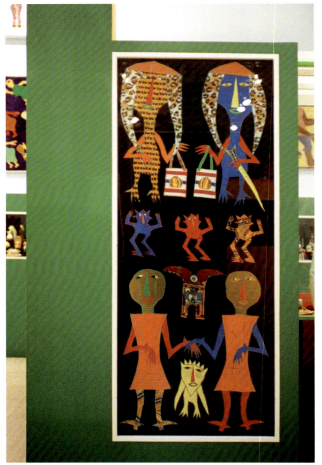

Displays housing Girard's folk art collection are clad in a variety of materials, including reclaimed unpainted wood and hand-painted panels, *Multiple Visions: A Common Bond*, Museum of International Folk Art, Santa Fe, New Mexico, 1981.

← Top: Circus-themed folk art tableau for HemisFair '68, San Antonio, Texas, 1968. Bottom: Girard-designed Spanish café tableau for *Multiple Visions: A Common Bond*, Museum of International Folk Art, Santa Fe, New Mexico, 1981.

→ *Multiple Visions: A Common Bond*, Museum of International Folk Art, Santa Fe, New Mexico, 1981. Top: Toy Shop tableau. Bottom: Processional tableau.

The largest of Girard's folk art shows was a permanent exhibition at the Museum of International Folk Art in Santa Fe, in 1981 (see pages 186–96). This exhibition was to be so expansive that Girard was also hired to design a whole new wing to house it. Here, Girard devised ways to beautifully accentuate his widely varied folk art. He constructed tiered stands, wall niches, display boxes, small staircases, and frames. He placed customized lighting everywhere and, of course, designed a timeless poster for the opening. In spite of being asked to place explanatory tags throughout the exhibition, he insisted on abstaining from this typical museum practice. He explained, "The average show tells the observer so much about the work on display that little time is left to look at it ... What we are trying to do is create an exhibition that will disturb and enchant the eye, rather than cram the viewer full of facts." Girard's exhibition designs from the 1960s to the 1980s show him bringing things together exquisitely to express his deep interest in how the people of the world reflected their human experience through the things they made.

Curating spaces wherein people could come to have an experience that sparked questions, challenged assumptions, or presented something familiar in a new way was the ultimate goal for Girard, and he did it time and time again.

Girard's interest in folk art started in childhood when he began collecting and assembling miniatures for Christmas creches. Professionally his love of folk art showed up in his very first interiors project: his home. In 1928, still an architecture student, Girard designed his own apartment in Florence, Italy. His preference for artisanal items was evident even in this early interior, where he placed handmade textiles from around the world, as well as sculptures and objects that he had collected. A few years later, in his 1935 New York City apartment (and then in every home afterward), he placed many folk art sculptures and ceramics. His continued inclusion of folk art was, in every instance, counter to the design trends of each period. At one of his Michigan studios in the 1940s, when most people had not traveled as extensively as Girard (and if they had, they were not seeking out the handcrafts he was doggedly after), he put on multiple public art shows of international folk art.

Girard always liked to travel—he was enthused by other cultures, other ways of life, and other languages (he spoke eight languages himself). He traveled as a young man, and then when he got married, he and his wife, Susan, traveled together. Later they were joined by their children. Girard was enthused by artwork that was not studied or erudite. He liked things that were, he said, "unsophisticated or naive in character; ingenious in concept; direct in expression; sincere in creation; bounded by the vigorous limitation of a tool, a material, a handcraft, or a machine process."

Girard's methods of selecting and collecting were fluid. While there were certainly instances when he was on a mission to find something specific, he was also open and willing to be surprised by another thing he may never have considered. Girard said, "Anything that smacks of 'you must have one of everything' is anathema to me." He had a way of walking through a market or a shop with a keen focus on even the smallest of details. Friends spoke of going through a grocery store with him and having the experience be as exciting as a museum visit when seeing the shelves through Girard's eyes. Nothing was taken for granted, and value was subjective.

Girard purchased folk art from every corner of the globe. He was an omnivore fueled not only by beauty but by commonalities in diverse cultures (a frog figurine of strikingly similar style and proportion might be found in Japan and in Egypt, made centuries apart). Girard was enthused by folk art everywhere he traveled, including Mexico, Guatemala, Brazil, Peru, Haiti, Poland, Sweden, Italy, India, Japan, Ethiopia, England, Spain, Germany, Portugal, and many other places. Girard's gift with languages helped his travels, but he often relied on a more foolproof way to find folk art in foreign countries: he held an item up to a taxi driver and asked where he could find things *like this.*

Over time, Girard built a collection of unique items that taken individually may have been quaint and perhaps even random, but all together, they started to become a lexicon of artifacts that reflected the many people and cultures from which they came. For example, you could take handmade models of boats from six seemingly disparate places around the globe and come to a deeper understanding of the human relationship with water. Every paper flower he selected, every papier-mâché doll, ceramic bird, beaded animal, castle, clay motorcycle, and naturally dyed weaving had a place in a larger context he was creating of how to see and understand the world we all inhabit. Through his presentations of these collections, he invited viewers to take in what they saw without having to know a great deal about it and react based on their own feeling and experience instead of some prescribed value.

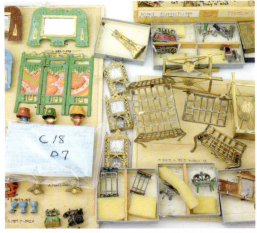

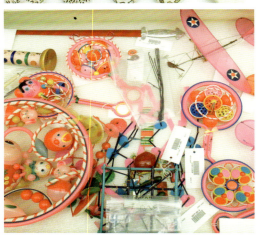

Textile designer Jack Lenor Larsen said, "The heart of the Girard collections is the very order of things that normally escape preservation."

Girard became an influential designer early in his career who was especially hard to copy. In the sphere of his collecting, Girard did not search for usual or categorizable things. When asked about the style of what he collected, he said:

> Style is not the thing which makes for individuality. Style is a way of getting rid of the responsibility of a thing. You, of course, can look at a piece of folk art and say, "Oh yes, Italian, thirteenth century." But what does this have to do with what you get out of it? Naturally, there are many obvious messages about the period in which the thing was done, but beyond that, you either like it or you don't. You can't explain why very well, and that causes you to look at the piece in greater depth—such as how it was done, the timbre of its expression, the timbre of a no longer existent voice. Of a no longer existent brain.

He added:

> That's a Giotto, so that must be good," we say, and we don't think anymore. It's finished. Folk art is not valuable in that dimension. Instead, it allows you to evaluate a whole new way of seeing things, of deciding on the worth of a piece for yourself. You're left holding the bag ... In true folk art, I do not think you can consider style; style is something you can copy. Or you can create a style that is new in comparison to what went before. Style can be broken, reevaluated, changed. But the folk artist, generally, is totally uneducated from such a point of view, so he doesn't have this problem, this great handicap. He creates out of himself directly, and as soon as he starts getting tampered with by outside influences, he no longer creates folk art.

When Girard moved from Michigan to New Mexico in 1953, modern design favored spare furnishings; the trend had moved away from having (for instance) too many keepsakes. Girard was a modern designer but saw the addition of folk art as a valuable juxtaposition that added a deeply human element to these otherwise restrained interiors. In his elegant houses, these small, handmade items brought earthiness, humor, and depth. The way he included them was intricate and artful, and was noticed by the larger design community. By the 1960s Girard had a monumental collection of figurines, sculptures, rugs, toys, masks, wall hangings, miniature plants, miniature castles, and more. Girard knew his passion for folk art was unusual. He once said, "What is wrong with me that I like this stuff?" Adding, "Somewhere here we are going to wind up using the word collector, and I want to say immediately that I don't care for the word at all. I don't really know what I could call it. It is more a matter of selecting than of collecting, and yet a selector sounds like something on a kitchen appliance." He also said, "To me it was really simple: love of the objects came first, and there was absolutely no other criterion for collecting."

Girard's use of folk art in his own residences spread outward to his clients and appeared in many of the homes he designed. While the ideal was for environments to be uncluttered, the reality was that, like Girard, many people owned quite a lot of stuff. Girard said, "It is absurd to store something beautiful in a closet simply because one has an ineptitude or a distaste for drilling holes in plaster." He was not being literal but asking everyone to stop following rules blindly. Not only did folk art pieces arrive in his clients' homes, Girard strikingly, irrepressibly, also placed them in his commercial interior projects. These included airport lounges, textile showrooms, and restaurants. In each instance, his design of these spaces was considered innovative and successful. People saw something exciting in what he was creating. Whether they realized it or not, he was holding a captivating conversation between modern design and ancient craftsmanship.

Of course, some entities missed Girard's elevated viewpoint and dismissed his interests in folk art as unsophisticated. In 1963 *Life* magazine wrote, "The country's most noted clutterbug is Alexander Girard." Girard disregarded that. He had found ways to make folk art sing in a wide range of settings, and through folk art, Girard was able to go even deeper than aesthetics and highlight human commonalities discovered by his incessant traveling. His love of and interest in these handmade objects, textiles, models, and toys grew alongside his career as a designer, and the two disciplines overlapped and influenced one another. He saw symbols in South and Central American folk art—as well as in that of India, China, and throughout Africa—that were still in rotation after hundreds of thousands of years. He adopted some of these into his own designs—snakes, birds, suns, spirals, checks, stars, eyes. In addition to accumulating the actual objects, he also spent time with the artisans themselves, and he treasured these relationships and what he was able to learn. Girard's folk art contribution was a lesson in global intersectionality, a history of human hands and minds.

In 1961 Girard built a fully fireproof five-thousand-square-foot cinder block room adjacent to his home in Santa Fe, New Mexico. This was called the Foundation,

which housed the collection that had become Girard's library of international folk art. The Foundation lent work to many exhibitions around the world, and Girard was invited to create a number of these shows himself. For one that took place in Santa Fe, he asked his friend, the artist Georgia O'Keeffe, to create miniature paintings for his tableaus. She did, but the museum couldn't afford to insure them (she was a highly collectible artist by then). Ultimately her paintings could not be shown, and they are possibly living out their days in a tiny humidity-controlled drawer. In 1978 Girard's Foundation was in possession of an extraordinary number of folk art pieces, and he donated many of them—106,000, to be precise—to the Museum of International Folk Art in Santa Fe, New Mexico.

A new wing was built at the Museum of International Folk Art to house and display Girard's collection. He designed the building himself. In 1981, with the structure complete, he debuted his permanent exhibition of folk art. For this show he created stunning displays chockfull of small human figures, animals, paintings, weavings, beadwork, and more. He built unique platforms and surrounds to highlight his arrangements. He added vernacular architecture in miniature to help carry each scenario—tiny sweeping arches, columns, prosceniums, storefronts, and store cabinets. He and his team built structures for a miniature café, a bullfight, a church, a shop, and a zocalo to name a few.

Girard's displays created such a seamless environment that a museumgoer might not realize where the folk art ended and Girard's display designs began. He said, "I've often felt that objects lose half their lives when taken out of their natural settings. To me, nothing could be worse than an exhibition in which a number of objects are just lined up in a case." One of Girard's assistants, Lesly Carr, said:

> It was a heck of a lot of fun as he was starting to prepare the transfer of things to the folk art museum; we actually started building some of the display pieces that are at the museum. And there's one in particular I remember—it was like a little Moroccan scene. And one day he said, "Are you going to be going to the store this weekend? Go someplace unusual and try and find different kinds of nuts and things." And so off I went, and I got nutmeg and all kinds of little seeds and what-notties. We sat there and painted some of those things to look like watermelons or whatever.

P. 192–193 Details from the exhibition featuring thousands of folk art pieces, *Multiple Visions: A Common Bond*, Museum of International Folk Art, Santa Fe, New Mexico, 1981.

P. 194 Girard installing the Spanish tableau for *Multiple Visions: A Common Bond*, Museum of International Folk Art, Santa Fe, New Mexico, 1981. Photograph by Charles Eames.

P. 195 Finished Spanish tableau, *Multiple Visions: A Common Bond*, Museum of International Folk Art, Santa Fe, New Mexico, 1981.

P. 196 Small sampling of archival storage of *Multiple Visions: A Common Bond*, Museum of International Folk Art, Santa Fe, New Mexico, 1981.

P. 198 Girard designed the exhibition poster for *The Magic of a People* at HemisFair '68 as well as the exhibition itself, HemisFair '68 World's Fair, San Antonio, Texas, 1968.

P. 199 The Girards in front of the slain devil at *The Magic of a People* exhibition, HemisFair '68 World's Fair, San Antonio, Texas, 1968.

← *The Magic of a People* exhibition at HemisFair '68 World's Fair, San Antonio, Texas, 1968. Top: Outside graphics. Bottom: Multicolored painted walls with metallic inlays clad the main entrance.

→ Multicolored ramps guide guests to and from *The Magic of a People* exhibition at HemisFair '68 World's Fair, San Antonio, Texas, 1968.

← *The Magic of a People* exhibition at HemisFair '68 World's Fair, San Antonio, Texas, 1968. Top: Entrance ramp with instructive angels reminding guests not to smoke or take photographs. Bottom: Painted tree of life.

→ Visitors followed a giant snake painted on the exterior of the building housing *The Magic of a People* exhibition at HemisFair '68 World's Fair, San Antonio, Texas, 1968.

At seventy-four, this was to be the magnum opus of Girard's career and the ultimate showcase for the trove of treasures he had spent a lifetime gathering. Girard designed an exhibit ripe with possibility and exploration. There was no "right" way to move through the space, and there was something to discover in every direction. With no explicit descriptions, viewers were left to follow their own innate sense of wonder, taking in the many scenes. Using the vast array of tools he had come to rely on when creating an interior—color, height, shape, texture, and lighting—Girard took each one to an exquisite extreme. He considered every type of person who might walk through and made sure there was something to be seen at every level. One could feel as if they were wandering the cobblestoned streets of a medieval village with a discovery around the corner, or perhaps down low, where they would have to bend to see it. There were spaces within spaces, things suspended from the ceiling, and hidden items to notice, making it a rich and layered exhibition one could visit repeatedly, each time observing something they had never seen before.

While in theory the density of the show could seem overwhelming, its execution was so precise that the sum of its parts created a visual symphony. Girard's studio assistant, Georgia Smith, talked about Girard visiting the show after its debut. She said, "I took him there many times. Coming from an art history background, I was always wanting things identified and classified, categorized, but Mr. Girard was like, 'It doesn't matter where it's from. Doesn't it look marvelous there?'" This encouragement of the viewer to experience the exhibition through whatever personal lens they brought was a token of faith in humanity. Girard was less interested in what people felt than he was that they felt something at all.

In 1968 Alexander Girard designed a striking exhibit at the World's Fair in San Antonio, Texas. The fair was called HemisFair, and its theme was "Confluence of Civilizations in the Americas." Girard titled his own contribution *El Encanto de un Pueblo* (which he translated as *The Magic of a People*; see pages 198–203). He mined his own vast collection of folk art for this exhibit, using pieces specifically from North and South America to fit the fair's theme. Girard created wondrous displays for HemisFair, and through his bold use of color and jumbo graphics, he delivered a complete transformation of the exterior of the building in which his exhibit was housed.

The concrete building Girard worked with at the World's Fair was a fairly plain piece of architecture: a few blocky rectangles set together. He transformed it by painting the exterior walls in large spans of bright colors. He painted different hues on every plane of a ramp going into and out of the exhibit. The effect was vivid and monumental (and it surely improved visitors' waiting experience outside). On the full sides of the building, Girard placed very highly saturated hues, one after another. The colors changed at every stopping point—wherever a wall turned ninety degrees or where the entrance jutted out. By doing this, Girard slimmed down the bulky architecture,

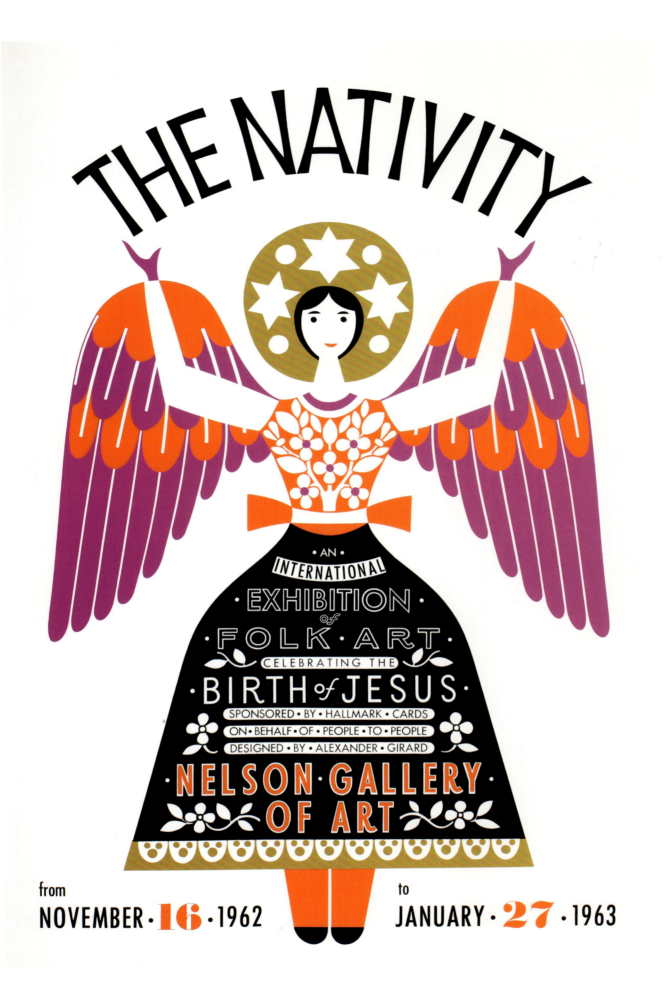

← Girard-designed poster for *The Nativity* exhibition, Nelson Gallery, Kansas City, Missouri, 1962.

→ Entrance design for *The Nativity*, Nelson Gallery, Kansas City, Missouri, 1962.

P. 206–207 Various Nativity displays from *The Nativity*, Nelson Gallery, Kansas City, Missouri, 1962.

reducing the perception of the building's volume. His exterior hues were astonishing and engaging—especially as backdrops to the oversized archetypes Girard added of an angel, a devil, a snake, a moon, a sun, and a tree of life. His vision was lush, and his building looked like no other at the fair. It also didn't look much like his own displays, which it housed. While Girard's building wore thick bands of color and large graphic shapes, the rooms inside held miniature, exceptionally intricate scenes. His displays of folk art were a spectacularly detailed dreamscape.

Inside his exhibit Girard lined the edges of the three-thousand-square-foot space with plentiful scenes of folk art. Each display was as intricate as an Elizabethan lace collar, full of literally hundreds of human figures, paper flowers, birds, and angels. A theatrical effect sprang not only from the charming color and craftsmanship of each piece (each was lovely and had been selected carefully), but Girard had built magic into his displays. His well-lit and extremely dense layering created something extraordinary. The effect of his glimmering row upon row of human and mythological figures and saints stacked together was stunning.

Girard used five thousand pieces of folk art among the displays. He depicted familiar stories with them, both real and imagined: One scenario portrayed the Garden of Eden; others showed a handcrafted hell, heaven, and Noah's Ark. The more ordinary settings were towns filled with folk art people, shops, a café. His miniature citizens gathered for a magnificent parade, a christening, a banquet, a cockfight, and a wake. Girard built miniature supports and environments for each of his arrangements—such as mountains, roads, and buildings to fit each theme. *El Abrazo* journal wrote, "Viewers will find themselves involved in the entire spectrum of life, communicated directly and simply. Here are humor, whimsy, tragedy and love." Because it was made by Girard, here also was display genius, stellar graphic design, and the largest example of his ability to integrate hundreds of objects together in an impactful tableau.

Though Girard had incorporated folk art into prestigious interior design projects for decades and had curated several well-regarded shows with it, some people still referred to the pieces he collected as *toys*. Many appreciated his HemisFair exhibit despite this, and praised his accomplishments with the "meager playthings." *El Abrazo* wrote, "Today these toys and other decorative objects communicate to us the powerful spirit of an emotional and imaginative people." One reporter bristled at the characterization writing, "To describe Girard's HemisFair collection as simply a toy collection is an understatement. The collection represented a whole depiction of life, fantasy, fear, superstition, hope, and

206 CURATION AND EXHIBITION DESIGN

religion." Girard himself certainly wasn't ruffled, as he had nothing against toys (in fact he collected quite a lot of them). His profound admiration for folk art, seen here and in many projects throughout his career, surely lingered long after the fair concluded and the exhibitions were disassembled.

In close succession, Alexander Girard curated two folk art shows titled *The Nativity*. The first was at the Museum of International Folk Art in Santa Fe, New Mexico, in 1961, and the second was at the Nelson Gallery in Kansas City, Missouri, in 1962 (see pages 204–207). Girard featured more than 150 Nativity creches in each show, including separate pieces he had assembled individually and full Nativity sets that he had collected whole. Each show displayed more than two thousand pieces of folk art. Girard first became interested in nativities as a child. After seeing creches in the churches of Italy, where he grew up, he began collecting his own figures and creating scenes from them.

In Girard's professional Nativity shows, each creche originated from a different country or culture. He said, "Seeing how each people, and each individual artist, depicts the same themes is an education in itself, one which cannot help but lead to greater understanding in the world." Not only did every Nativity come from a different group of people, Girard made sure each showed a different style, was made of different materials, and appeared unique in character. He helped keep each distinct by designing changing platforms, complementary frames, wreaths, niches, domes, and tiered and stepped surrounds. Girard suspended a low, dark ceiling across the exhibit spaces to create a feeling of night. The displays were described as being "placed with architectural, Mondrian-like precision. Tiny windows hold the wee groups that would not cover the palm of the hand."

Because Girard wanted viewers to focus on their experience more than the provenance of each item, he placed no opening statements on the walls of the shows and included scant information about each creche. While this was not intended to deprive any artisan of credit for their work, it left the viewer with an opportunity to consider the exhibit without prescribed value or origin. He designed beautiful catalogs for the Nativity shows that included no text. He had curated many shows before and had seen viewers reach for facts that only worked to distract them from looking deeply and feeling things out for themselves. It was also Girard trying to remove bias between cultures. He included a wall of text in one Nativity show that was a lovely graphic of words and phrases that expressed his theme in many languages—words such as *Nativity, creche, stable,* and *Bethlehem* in Portuguese, German, Ukrainian, and more. He painted these in his own highly decorative typeface. While Girard was not a religious man in practice, he was fascinated by symbols and concepts that could transcend language, borders, and cultures. Anytime Girard could build a bridge through the visual to make connections where there otherwise may not be one, he took full advantage.

Letterforms

ALEXANDER GIRARD'S PASSION FOR languages, both spoken and written, was born at an early age. Growing up in a bilingual house sparked his interest in the concept of communication, and by the end of his life he had learned to speak eight languages. This fascination took him beyond the Roman alphabet into the letterforms of Russian, Chinese, Japanese, and Sanskrit. Combining this interest with his meticulous draftsman skills, he created his own collection of typefaces and graphics throughout his vast career. He considered the letterform an important facet in any project he undertook, as it could be a powerful extension of the overall design concept and another way to deliver whatever story he was trying to tell.

He occasionally took on solitary graphic design jobs, but more typically his graphics came as an added benefit to projects for which he was hired as an interior designer; textile, furniture, or product designer; curator; or general mastermind. To all of those clients Girard delivered unanticipated and exceptional graphic designs. Starting with the small exhibitions at his own design studios and then throughout the entirety of his career, Girard created custom type and graphic solutions, including posters, menus, wall graphics, invitations, sales brochures, stationery, and signage. He received accolades for several of his innovative and beautiful graphic inventions.

"usic"

1955
4 embroidered linens
9 printed linens
3 glazed percales
9 worsted
many unusual stripes
& other things

305 east 63 new york october 27 & thereafter

ics signed by alexander girard for the herman miller tion

Girard's graphic work was uniquely adaptive to each customer and theme. It was also full of invention. He disregarded industry standards by combining many typefaces and font sizes within one work. On his posters for two Herman Miller showrooms (Barbary Coast and Textiles & Objects), Girard mixed block and cursive letters. For the Textiles & Objects poster he printed his design on a hand-printed paper whose rough texture contrasted his clean, mostly modernist typefaces. Girard was whimsically unpredictable with kerning (something no one would have advised, but in his hands, surprisingly, it made his text more readable).

A friend once said, "Sandro Girard's secret is really very simple. He retains the eye of a child." Studio Assistant Karl Tani said about Girard's graphics:

> He had a very unorthodox way of approaching things. I mean, I teach typography and graphic design, and there are certain kinds of rules about type I've kind of been ingrained with. But Mr. Girard was able to break out of that kind of stuff. When he designed the Compound restaurant in Santa Fe, he would use a sans serif type with a serif type of thing, then a curlicue on the end. All of the kind of stuff you wouldn't think would work. It doesn't make sense, but it worked … You could never make it into an alphabet that would work, because the letters wouldn't relate. But then as a design, it worked.

A few of Girard's graphic designs were especially praised. The Textiles & Objects poster achieved iconic success despite (or because of) its deviation from classical typographic rules. Girard's graphics for Braniff International Airways also stood out—not just his chic Braniff logo but the many variations of it he created and placed on all of its paper goods. For some of Girard's typefaces, he created full alphabets, but more commonly, he drew only enough letters to enable one design. The latter was true of his textile pattern *Names*, made from letters in the names of Herman Miller executives. It was also true of his door design for the Scoren residence, where Girard's composition (made from letters in their name) was printed in bright squares and stood out like a boisterous welcome flag.

Girard did not approach graphic design as a chore; it was more something he could not keep away from. During his detailed design of the interior of a home belonging to Irwin and Xenia Miller, he found time to create a complementary logo for Xenia that interlocked her name with her husband's in clever tango postures. Closer to home, Girard designed numerous graphics that were playful, loving blends of the letters in his nickname, Sandro, and his wife's name, Susan. These explorations were visual expressions of devotion.

While Girard's graphics often succeeded because of his facility with text, his designs ultimately triumphed because they were equally expressive in pace, layout, and coloring. *Interiors* magazine wrote about Girard, "It is the inventive imagination of Alexander Girard's that we continuously admire." Jack Lenor Larsen wrote, "Girard is a humanist, a student of the visual forces that move people and especially of those that delight." Many of Girard's graphic designs manage to avoid seeming outdated even after as many as sixty years. His facility and innovation continue to reach out and inspire.

P. 208–209 Girard designed the poster announcement for his new textile collection for Herman Miller, silkscreen on tissue, 1955.

← Girard designed the poster announcement for the new Herman Miller San Francisco showroom, 1958.

→ Top: Sketches for Girard wedding anniversary designs, 1976. Bottom: Graphic sketch for the Miller Home and Garden, featuring the intertwined first names of the homeowners, Irwin and Xenia, 1953.

← Top: *Seviche* sketch for La Fonda del Sol, 1960. Middle and bottom: Sketches of letterform studies for barware, 1930s.

→ Top: Swirling exploration of Susan and Sandro's names together, 1950s. Middle: Type study for Amistad project. Bottom: Developmental sketches for the invitation to the Girard-designed Environmental Enrichment Panels collection, 1972.

← Studies for Girard wedding anniversary designs, 1970s.

→ Top and middle: Girard-designed typeface sketch and refinement, 1940s. Bottom: Land protection poster, 1970s.

BREAKFAST		LUNCH	
special		1 enchilada	1-50
creamed chipped beef on toast	1-25	2 enchilada with egg	1-65
1 two fried eggs	-75	3 burrito bean	-65
2 two eggs bacon, ham or sausage	1-30	4 burrito meat	-75
3 ham omelet	1-00	5 tacos (two)	-50
4 cheese omelet	-85	6 bowl of chile	-70
5 plain omelet	-75	7 hamburger	-70
6 huevos rancheros	1-40	8 cheeseburger	-80
7 large stack 4 pancakes	-80	9 grilled cheese sandwich	-45
8 small stack 3 pancakes	-60	10 ham sandwich	-75
9 french toast	-80	11 ham and cheese sandwich	-85
* nos: 2, 3, 4, 5 served with fried potatoes, toast and jelly		12 bacon, lettuce & tomato	-75

dry cereal	-35	coffee	-15	hot dog	-35
donut	-20	tea	-15	chile dog	-45
toast	-20	milk	-15 or -20	tortillas	-10
side/one egg	-35	hot chocolate	-20	sopaipillas	-10
side/bacon, ham or sausage	-50	sodas	-15	side/chile	-10
		juice	-15		

← Top, left: Sketch for logo for the Compound, Santa Fe, New Mexico, 1966. Top, right: Type developmental sketch, 1940s. Bottom: Hand-painted menu for Marshall Girard's hamburger stand, 1970s.

→ Top: L'Etoile repeat sketch, 1965. Bottom: Susan and Sandro interlocking pattern exploration, 1950s.

AFRICAN FABRICS

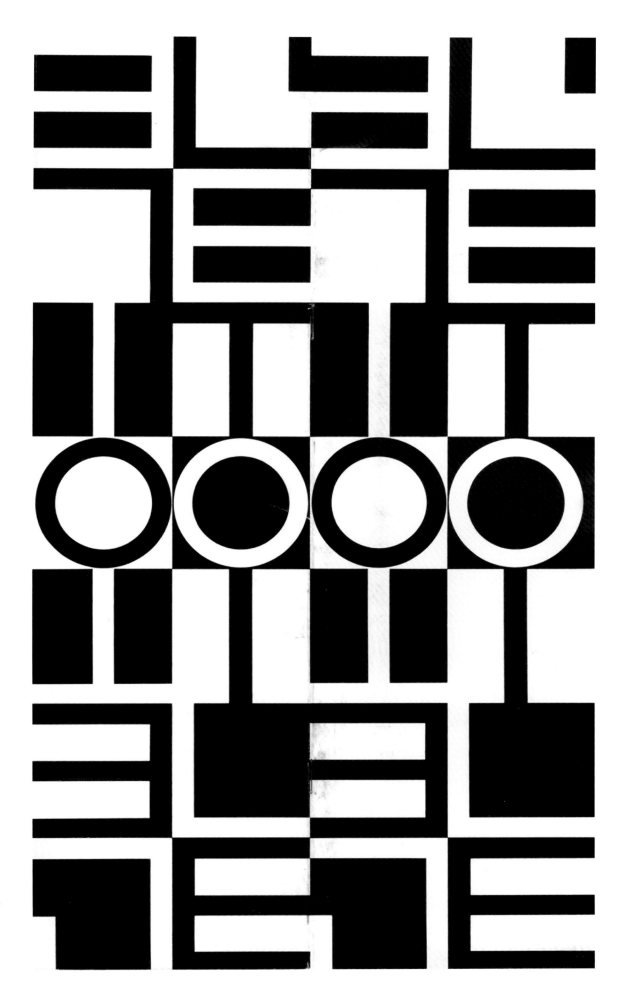

← Painting of type for *African Fabrics* exhibition of Girard's textile collection, Museum of International Folk Art, Santa Fe, New Mexico, 1975.

→ L'Etoile restaurant menu painting, 1965.

a division of
herman miller inc.
zeeland, mich.

8 east · **53**
new york city

Textiles
&
Objects

designed or selected
by alexander girard

← Girard-designed poster for the Textiles & Objects shop, 1961.

→ Girard-designed L'Etoile beer bottle and sugar packets, 1966.

Restaurants

ON A FEW OCCASIONS, ALEXANDER
Girard contributed only minimal aspects to a restaurant design—murals and wall reliefs in the Passy Restaurant in 1934, murals in Café Trouville in 1935, and a set of large metal characters in Le Pavillon in 1962. However, as was his preference, Girard had the opportunity to take on the entire interior design of four very different restaurants from 1937 to 1966: Charles' a la Pomme Soufflee, La Fonda del Sol, L'Etoile, and the Compound. The environment of each one varied greatly in character and tone, but they all spoke Girard-ese. In each restaurant, Girard addressed large matters first—he optimized the layout, identified furniture needs, and chose colors and surface materials. After that, when many designers considered their projects nearly done, he really got started. Girard had always brimmed with ideas, and he often overstepped the traditional role of an interior designer. In his restaurant projects, he could often not help but design a new logo and menu. He had too many concepts not to create custom lighting and furniture, original wall art, and sometimes dinnerware as well. The *New Yorker* magazine called one of his restaurant projects "Alexander Girard's museum." Girard's designs encompassed so many of his interests, the description was not entirely off the mark.

P. 222–223 Etched glass wall in L'Etoile, New York City, 1965. Photograph by Charles Eames.

Design details from L'Etoile featuring enameled daisy tables and Girard chairs in red, white, and blue upholstery, 1966. Photographs by Charles Eames.

← View from entrance of L'Etoile to flower-shaped dessert display and faceted lamps, 1966. Photograph by Charles Eames.

→ Top: Upstairs dining at L'Etoile, featuring dynamic jacquard wall panels in multiple colorways, 1966. Photograph by Charles Eames. Bottom: Girard-designed folding menu for L'Etoile, 1966.

Alexander Girard's first restaurant design, in 1937, was Charles' a la Pomme Soufflee in New York City. It was not a grandiose endeavor, but it was elegant, clever, and shows many of Girard's genes. Since no color images of the interior exist (very few images survive at all), one clue about Girard's designs appears in a quote from *Vogue* magazine: "In the long upper room of this restaurant, the walls are punctuated with large-scale relief and brightly coloured." That small mention of color is an early indicator of Girard's tendency to use bold hues (something he later became known for). The reliefs being referred to were distinctive plaster sculptures Girard created, without being asked, that graced the restaurant walls. Above them hung his custom lighting, another element Girard designed without anyone requesting it. In one of Charles' a la Pomme Soufflee's dining rooms there was a center row of dining tables with their points lined up like diamonds rather than squares (this was a recognizable Girard touch and something he would later repeat at the Compound). In the terrazzo floor, Girard laid the stone in colored stripes—a gesture he would perform again in the Michigan cafeteria of the Detrola Headquarters with linoleum. While the designs at Charles' a la Pomme Soufflee were restrained, they were no less Girard works than any others.

In 1960 Alexander Girard designed a brand-new New York City restaurant called La Fonda del Sol. Unlike his design of the modest Charles' a la Pomme Soufflee more than twenty years earlier, La Fonda arrived full of design swagger. The project was a remarkably gargantuan undertaking, during which Girard chose to reconfigure the flow of rooms and design most of the furniture, all of the lighting, the restaurant's logo, and gobs of colorful wall graphics. He created custom dinnerware for La Fonda, too, which included plates, cups, bowls, coffee makers, glasses, and saltshakers. He also put his hand to designing small elements such as door pulls, sink faucets, and napkins. He used bright colors and patterns, piled up textures, and added bold signage. Girard brought on an avant-garde fashion designer to create uniforms for the waitstaff. La Fonda del Sol was a rich environment that appeared on the scene with a bang; its loud color and overall muchness were noticed. Many reviewers mentioned Girard's work at La Fonda more than they did the food.

Alexander Girard's last two restaurants, L'Etoile (see pages 222–27) and the Compound (see pages 232–35), were designed in 1966. Both had subtler design schemes than his usual. After La Fonda del Sol and many subsequent densely colorful projects, the change in tone was feasibly refreshing for Girard. Or possibly he simply seized the opportunity to show his breadth. Though L'Etoile and the Compound were created in the same year, each had a physique of its own: where L'Etoile was urban and refined, winking with small lights and etched glass panels, the Compound had an earthy posture and sported a coved ceiling where thick layers of plaster were applied over the beams of the roof structure. While it was typical in adobe architecture to leave these beams exposed as wooden elements, Girard painted everything white, creating a modern, wavelike plane. Neither treatment—at L'Etoile or the Compound—

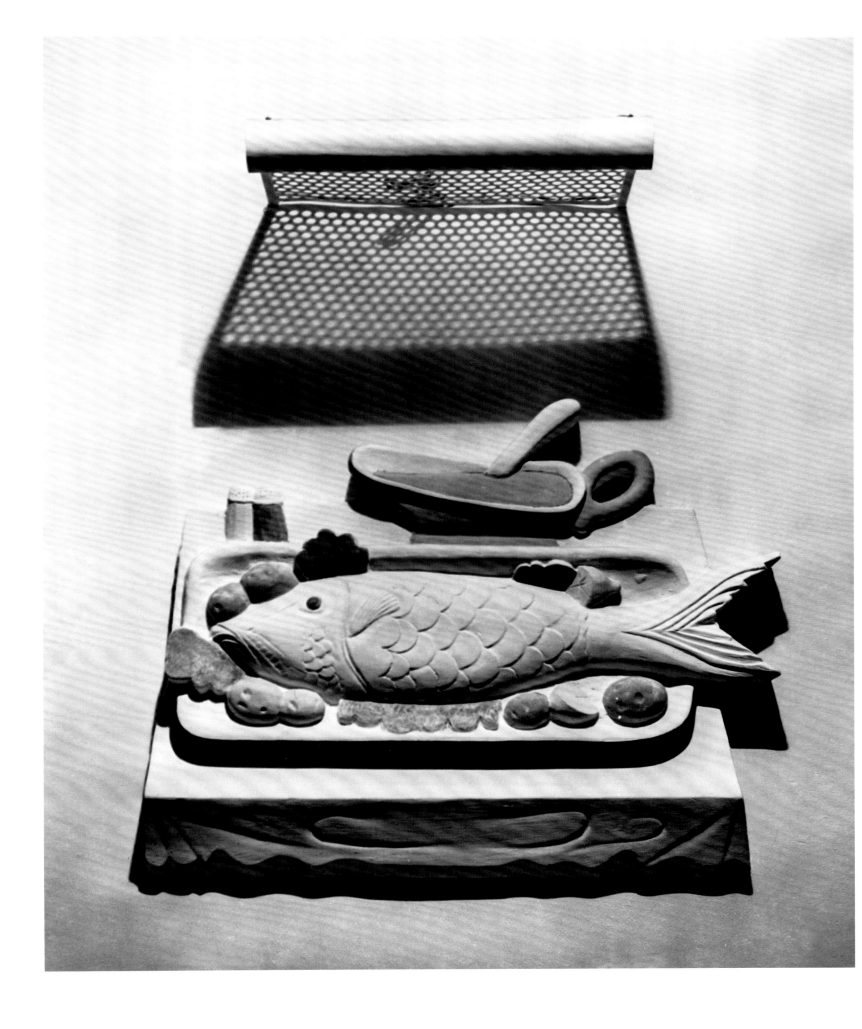

P. 228 Dining room at Charles' a la Pomme Soufflee with striped terrazzo floor, New York City, 1937.

P. 229 Plaster relief with custom lighting at Charles' a la Pomme Soufflee, New York City, 1937.

Girard explored murals featuring dramatic, soaring architectural scenes over the years, location unknown, 1930s.

was dull or expected, and both showed Girard's mastery over texture and shape.

The message at L'Etoile, situated in New York City, was one of elegance and refinement. Girard said of L'Etoile, "It will be a total antithesis of La Fonda." It was, and it wasn't. The decibel of Girard's design was quieter, but the totality of his vision remained unchanged. Girard designed a new font for L'Etoile, new signage, and a new menu. He created custom lighting, display furniture, seating, carpets, and metal balustrades. His design scheme was mostly in neutral colors of black, brown, and silver, which was highly unusual. He included star symbols to reflect the restaurant's name—appearing subtly in etched glass panels and a gleaming chandelier. The loudest addition to L'Etoile might have been Girard's fantastical flowerlike structure—more sculpture than furniture—that was used to present desserts.

Girard created distinct dining areas within L'Etoile's footprint and assigned exclusive details to each. The bar sat a few steps higher than the dining room, and it had Girard's custom-designed daisy-shaped tables. The bar had the same chairs Girard had placed elsewhere in the restaurant, but here, he upholstered them in red, white, and blue to reference the French flag. A writer for *Interiors*, describing more typically designed French restaurants, wrote of the diners at L'Etoile, "It is Girard whom they have to thank for not having to dine under red damask and gold leaf." Girard hadn't fallen prey to the trend. He truly never embraced a timeline other than his internal one.

Soon after his design of L'Etoile, that same year, Alexander Girard took on the design of the Compound restaurant in Santa Fe, New Mexico. Taking cues from the shapes of the adobe structure as well as the local aesthetics of Santa Fe, Girard again found himself transforming an existing space into something completely new. Along flat areas of the Compound's ceilings, Girard installed a number of textile-based patchwork collages. He also made sure to include some of his favorite archetypal symbols but created them anew for this space. A brass sun and moon hung over two different dining nooks, a twenty-foot rainbow arched over a doorway to the outside patio, and a snake painted on the ceiling undulated over the coved beams. Girard also created a new iteration of his *International Love Heart* graphic in the form of a hand-painted wooden sign that greeted diners at the entrance. He installed his own textiles over *bancos* (adobe benches) and, of course, pillows for comfort when sitting against the wall. He placed the bar a few steps lower than the dining room this time, rather than above it as he had at L'Etoile. As he did in his other restaurants, Girard redrew the Compound's logo and menu, napkins, and matchbook covers. In the back room he created an altar of miniature food housed in a perfectly lit vitrine, once again incorporating his love of folk art and the handmade. On one dining room wall Girard hung a custom painting of his own that portrayed diners sitting at a table, on the corner of which he painted a mouse. Mouse was Girard's family nickname, so its position acted as a signature. It also served as a reminder that throughout Girard's commissions, he infused every project with its own flavor but always found a way—whiskered or not—to be himself.

← Mirror-finish moon and star with coved ceiling in the Compound, Santa Fe, New Mexico, 1966

↑ Handmade brass sun shines on the adobe-walled interior of the Compound, Santa Fe, New Mexico, 1966.

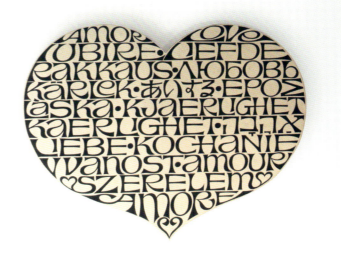

← Detail of patchwork vintage handwoven blankets lining the ceiling at the Compound, Santa Fe, New Mexico, 1966.

↑ Cutout, painted wooden panels throughout the Compound restaurant, Santa Fe, New Mexico, 1966.

La Fonda del Sol

IN 1960 ALEXANDER GIRARD WAS HIRED to design a new Latin American–themed restaurant in the Time and Life building in New York City. It was called La Fonda del Sol. As a first step in the design process, Girard embarked on multiple research trips throughout Central and South America, gathering inspiration. Coalescing everything he had seen and putting it through his own design filter, Girard created an amalgamation of the many locales he had traveled through. This process resulted in one of the first themed restaurants in New York City—not wholly of one country, cuisine, or culture but instead a fantasy interior based around reverence to the universal symbol of the sun. Girard said, "La Fonda del Sol, in its totality, is an abstract symbol of Latin America, a special 'stage world' and not a historically or realistically accurate reproduction of any given place or prototype."

Girard's curiosity led him to gain a deep understanding of each place he traveled through. He not only gathered visual inspiration and folk art but also the history of the people, their language, and their crafts. He drafted eighty different sun designs after noticing the pre-Columbian symbol was still prevalent throughout Latin America. He drew his in hot colors and added them to La Fonda's bar carts, waitstaff uniforms, menus, mugs, matchbooks, and even the wrappings around the restaurant's sugar cubes. Girard brought volumes of folk art back from his trip, including figurines, ceramic pots, stringed instruments, Day of the Dead skeletons, and brass suns. He arranged most of these at La Fonda in niches he built into the walls.

P. 236–237 Make-ready printing sheet for the matchbooks for La Fonda del Sol, New York City, 1960.

↑ Girard's painting for the tilework behind the kitchen for La Fonda del Sol, New York City, 1960.

¡BIENVENIDOS!

Esta casa é sua... Sejam Bemvindos a LA FONDA DEL SOL, pois aqui encontrarão variedades de cores e costumes como nos paízes sulamericanos.

Venham, portanto, saborear as nossas especialidades, típicos preparados como se fazem nas fazendas e solares dos paízes onde brilha o sol da América Latina.

Gratos pela preferência!

WELCOME!

"This is your house"... In this spirit of hospitality, we welcome you to LA FONDA DEL SOL.

Here in an atmosphere reflecting all the color, folklore and gaiety of our neighbors to the South, we invite you to enjoy food as it is prepared in the Haciendas and Inns of all the countries under the Latin American Sun.

Good Appetite!

¡BIENVENIDO!

Está usted en su casa . . . LA FONDA DEL SOL extiende a usted junto con sus saludos, toda su hospitalidad.

En esta atmósfera que refleja el folklore, color y alegría de nuestros vecinos, les invitamos a gustar los platos típicos preparados como en las haciendas y fondas de todos los países bajo el Sol Latinoamericano.

¡Buen Apetito!

WHISKIES

Escocés, Regular *Scotch*		1.00
Escocés, Superior *Premium Scotch*		1.15
Canadienses e Irlandeses *Canadian and Irish*		1.15
Americanos *Rye and Bourbon*		1.00
Americanos, Garantidos *Bonded Whiskies*		1.15

LICORES

Tres Cepas, Pedro Domecq	1.00
Fundador, Pedro Domecq	1.00
Anís del Mono	1.00
Bobadilla Ojén	1.00
Tía María	1.00
Torrente Ananá	1.00
Torrente Banana	1.00
Crema de Xtabentun	1.00
Kahlua	1.00
Crema de Café	1.00
Crema de Cacao	1.00
Crema de Menta, Helada	1.00

Además todos los licores mas famosos del mundo

CERVEZAS

Carta Blanca	.75	Balboa	.75
Moctezuma	.75	Cristal	.75
Superior	.75	Indio	.75
Bohemia Ale	.75	Cervezas Nacionales	.60
Fonda Chopp	.50		

REFRESCOS

Mango Punch	.50
Gingerberry Soda	.50
Tamarindo Fizz	.50

BEBIDAS MIXTAS TÍPICAS

Pisco Sawer *Peruvian Brandy Sour*	1.15
Tequila con Sangrita *Tequila Straight · Chaser · Lime · Salt*	1.00
Margarita *Tequila · Cointreau · Lime · Salt Frost*	1.15
Sangría María *Tequila · Mexican Tomato Juice*	1.25
Coctél del Mono *Anise · Cognac · Lime · Bitters*	1.25
Taxco Fizz *Mescal · Lime · Sugar · Egg*	1.15
San Martín, Seco *Martini, Very Dry*	1.00
Algarrobina Coctél *Pisco · Peruvian Herbs · Lime*	1.15
Champaña-Ananá *Champagne Cocktail with Pineapple*	1.65
Coctél Alegría *Pisco · Cointreau · Apricot Brandy*	1.25

Manzanilla .75	Jerez .75

BEBIDAS con RON

Batida *Cachaça · Lime · Sugar*	1.15
Mojito Criollo *Rum · Lime · Crushed Mint*	1.00
Floridita *Lime · Rum · Maraschino*	1.00
Daiquirí Clásico *White Rum · Lime · Sugar*	1.00
Maté y Caña *Lime · Rum · Pineapple Liqueur · Cha Mate*	1.25
Mezcla de Ron y Café *Rum · Sugar · Coffee · Cinnamon Bark*	1.25
Coctél Dorado *White Rum · Honey · Lime*	1.00

VINOS · WINES · VINHOS

Blancos · White · Brancos

MÉXICO
Bodegas Miramar – 1/1 Botella 3.25 – 1/2 Botella 1.75
PERÚ
Vista Alegre – 1/1 Botella 3.75 – 1/2 Botella 2.00
BRASIL
Dreher Riesling – 1 Garrafa 2.25
CHILE
Undurraga Rhin – 1/1 Botella 2.50 – 1/2 Botella 1.25
Undurraga Sauvignon Reservado – 1/1 Botella 1.25
San Pedro Riesling – 1/1 Botella 2.50
ARGENTINA
Cruz del Sur – 1/1 Botella 3.75
Cruz de Lorena – 1/1 Botella 3.75
ESPAÑA
Marqués de Murrieta – 1/1 Botella 4.50 – 1/2 Botella 2.75

Tintos · Red · Tintos

MÉXICO
Bodegas Miramar – 1/1 Botella 3.25 – 1/2 Botella 1.75
PERÚ
Vista Alegre – 1/1 Botella 3.75 – 1/2 Botella 2.00
BRASIL
Dreher Borbonha – 1 Garrafa 2.25
CHILE
San Pedro Borgoña – 1/1 Botella 2.50
Undurraga Pinot – 1/1 Botella 2.50 – 1/2 Botella 1.25
Undurraga Cabernet Reservado – 1/1 Botella 2.25
ARGENTINA
Rodas Borgoña – 1/1 Botella 3.25
Carcassonne Cabernet – 1/1 Botella 3.25
Cuevas de Vera – 1/1 Botella 3.25
ESPAÑA
Marqués de Riscal – 1/1 Botella 4.50 – 1/2 Botella 2.75

Rosado · Rose · Rosado

MÉXICO
Bodegas Miramar – 1/1 Botella 3.25 – 1/2 Botella 1.75

Espumosos · Sparkling · Espumosos

ARGENTINA
Tardieu Brut – 1/1 Botella 6.25
Tardieu Demi Sec – 1/1 Botella 6.00
Tardieu Sec – 1/1 Botella 6.00
CHILE
Valdivieso – 1/1 Botella 6.50

Sidra · Cider · Sidra

ESPAÑA
El Gaitero – 1/1 Botella 4.00 – 1/2 Botella 2.25

SANGRÍA · WINE PUNCH · SANGRÍA

Blanca o Roja	White or Red	Branca ou Tinta
1/1 Botella 3.25	Bottle 3.25	1 Garrafa 3.25
1/2 Botella 1.75	1/2 Bottle 1.75	1/2 Garrafa 1.75

Folding menu for La Fonda del Sol, New York City, 1960. Restaurant guests were encouraged to take the menus and mail them to friends and loved ones.

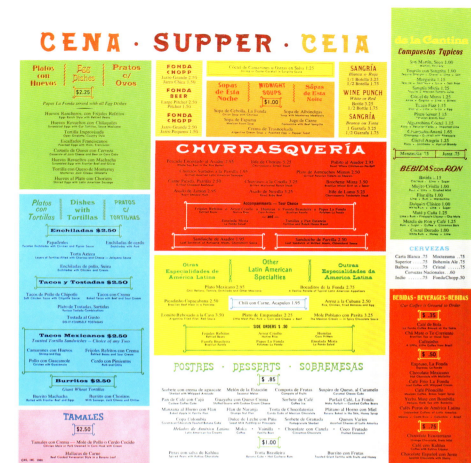

Front and back of the supper menu designed by Girard for La Fonda del Sol, New York City, 1960.

← Girard's sketches for La Fonda del Sol tableware, New York City, 1960.

→ Plaster models made for La Fonda del Sol tableware, New York City, 1960.

← Finished porcelain and linen tableware for La Fonda del Sol, New York City, 1960.

→ Glassware for La Fonda del Sol, New York City, 1960.

← Top: Exposed kitchen at La Fonda del Sol with painted tile back wall, 1960. Bottom: La Fonda del Sol dining room detail with giant brass sun and lowered-back Eames chairs, 1960. Photographs by Charles Eames.

→ A lively main dining room at La Fonda del Sol, New York City, 1960.

The uniforms at La Fonda del Sol were designed by Rudi Gernreich and featured Girard's textiles and gold bullion embroidery, New York City, 1960. Photograph by Charles Eames.

Private dining room with niches at La Fonda del Sol, New York City, 1960. Photograph by Charles Eames.

Design details in La Fonda del Sol, including custom door pulls, guacamole carts, and multicolored sugar cube wrappers, New York City, 1960. Photographs by Charles Eames.

← Enclosed adobe dining areas at La Fonda del Sol, New York City, 1960.

→ La Fonda del Sol, New York City, 1960. Top: Front entrance of La Fonda del Sol with custom type design. Bottom: Central dining area with embroidered umbrella.

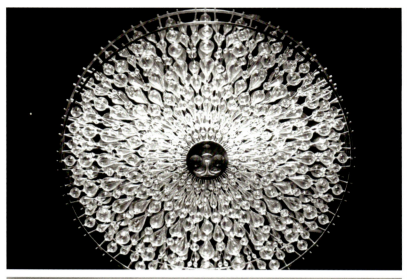

La Fonda del Sol, New York City, 1960. Clockwise from top left: handblown glass sun over the main entrance, Girard's architectural model of La Fonda del Sol, custom beer pitcher, front door logo, and Girard-designed coffee service.

Girard's design of La Fonda offered an especially vivid profusion of pattern and color. He placed intricate murals on the walls, put brightly colored graphics on menus and signage, and added accompanying wall text (see pages 238–41). He placed bold colors on carts, dinnerware, and uniforms and quieter colors on La Fonda's walls, pulling from a palette that a portrait painter might use—roses, beiges, straws (see pages 248–51). The New Yorker said about La Fonda del Sol, "You might be too interested in your surroundings to concentrate on your escort."

La Fonda del Sol was more like a multi-act opera than an interiors assignment. Girard created a variety of distinct dining experiences within its walls. It was his clever solution to an awkward floor plan that comprised a string of poorly connected rooms. The result of Girard's design was not chaotic but magical. As many designers know, presenting a range of ideas while retaining unity requires mastery. Girard accomplished this. He employed design embellishments and freestanding structures to differentiate seating areas. A giant embroidered canopy encapsulated one dining zone. Another was demarcated by a low brick wall, yet another by a large metal sun sculpture. One small dining room sat inside an adobe cube, its walls almost black, its ceiling upholstered in checked fabric. Girard's use of so many designs fit miraculously into his own unified whole. It inspired excitement in diners, many of whom found their preferred spot and returned to it. Textile designer Jack Lenor Larsen said, "The success of La Fonda whetted our appetite for more romantic, diversified interiors."

Another innovation that thrilled and impressed all who came to La Fonda del Sol was the open kitchen. Chefs and their assistants worked at a giant checked counter with a massive wall of custom-painted type as the backdrop (see pages 238–39 and 246). Girard—employing his mastery of fonts, language, and colors—conceived of this treatment as a nod to the incredible signage he had observed throughout his travels and an education in the restaurant's cuisine. Unlike other fine dining of the time, where the chefs, ingredients, and cooking process were hidden away, this stagelike atmosphere created a feast for all the senses and a conversation between the many people working to make the food and those who enjoyed it. The breakdown to this barrier allowed for an exciting honesty in the dining experience that wouldn't become a regular feature in restaurants until the 1980s.

Almost every stick of furniture in La Fonda del Sol was of Girard's design, but when it came to seating for the restaurant, Girard turned to his friend Charles Eames, whose handsome fiberglass chair was very popular. Girard loved Eames's chair, but its height blocked the dining tables, which Girard wanted to keep visible so he asked Eames if he would design a custom version of his chair for La Fonda with a lower back. Eames complied. In addition to this modification, the two designers collaborated on a new base to make the chair sturdier for such a high-traffic, commercial setting.

Calling on another colleague, Girard asked Los Angeles fashion designer Rudi Gernreich to create uniforms for the waitstaff of La Fonda. Gernreich designed these using Girard's textile designs, and all of the uniforms were stylish and colorful. One maître d' poncho included beautiful gold embroidery on its front. It was a piece of impressive artistry, even if it might have been impractical for restaurant work.

Girard did not cut corners when creating custom dinnerware for La Fonda, he did not print his logo on existing pieces; instead he designed each item himself, working from sketch to plaster prototype to final form. The tableware was remarkable. It encompassed plates and bowls, glasses, mugs, creamers, sugar bowls, oil and vinegar bottles, salt and pepper shakers, match strikes, and match holders (see pages 242–44). Girard designed different glasses for beer, sangria, and tequila, with corresponding pitchers for each (see page 245). He designed a coffee maker that came to a diner's table, its brewing process visible through glass. He placed a sun symbol on a few of the dinnerware pieces and used a cheerful range of colors on others, but the colors were used as accents, appearing, for example, only on the bottom of a glass or just on one ring of a mug.

At La Fonda, Girard seemed to consistently feel out and find the proper weight for everything. He worked intentionally and then reached intuitively for the place where all details became complementary to each other. Looking at the dinnerware separate from the raucous environment of La Fonda, it was an elegantly adaptable design that would not compete with anything nearby. Each separate element of Girard's overall design amplified one vision. Jack Lenor Larsen said of La Fonda, "The most important statement, more durable than the totality of the planning, the props, or the color, was the assertion that the prime concern of any environmental design was how people feel in a space. This is Girard's message and main contribution."

Commercial Interiors

ALEXANDER GIRARD DESIGNED A significant number of commercial interiors over many decades. He created highly customized, novel spaces for restaurants, offices, showrooms, stores, hotels, motels, and more. His projects collectively reveal some of his unswerving tastes—a love of graphic design and unusual textiles, rapt attention to color and lighting—but each of Girard's designs was otherwise distinct; he had a gigantic toolbox and used it capably. Almost as soon as Girard moved to New York from Florence, Italy, in 1932, his interior design skills became obvious. In 1934 he designed one room in a decorative arts and crafts exhibition at Rockefeller Center (see pages 284–85). Vogue called it "a room so unusual that on one visit you can hardly absorb the dozens of ideas it incorporates."

In the 1930s Girard took on many interior projects, including the New York City restaurants Passy Restaurant, Café Trouville, and Charles' a la Pomme Soufflee. He also accepted a couple of small jobs in Michigan, where he had recently moved. It was uncommon for him to put his hand to any space without taking over every inch of it, reimagining a company's presence from logo to furniture and beyond. So these smaller commissions stand out for their modesty and act as proof that Girard could be restrained in scope while still injecting an environment with great style.

Girard undertook the first of these smaller jobs in 1938 when he remade the interior of a Michigan store that sold goods made by disabled people called the Junior League Little Shop. Girard's wife, Susan, had a friend who worked there, which is how the designer came to be involved. It was undoubtedly rare for a shop this modest to work with such a distinguished designer. Girard painted the ceiling of the shop a bright rose and the walls mauve. He designed a very pretty modern chest of drawers (that would look contemporary in a store even today) to hold needlepoint samplers for sale. He built display shelves that echoed the shop's curved front window. He also designed a remarkable logo for the sign out front.

In 1939 Girard took on the second modest project in Michigan, creating transformative displays for a temporary market called the Women's Exchange Fair (see pages 256–57 and 259). Here Girard tackled the problem of an exhibition space with such imposing architecture it dwarfed the exhibit tables inside. He designed and painted dynamic large display boards to frame each table. These worked to unify and enlarge the tables' presence and put attention onto the merchandise rather than the cavernous space around it. Girard's signage was inventive; it contained everything interesting about the space. He designed large plywood borders for each table composed of his own leaf and flower patterns and lovely custom lettering. Each of his illustrations was intricate and lively.

Throughout the 1940s and 1950s Girard delivered unusually customized interiors again and again. He designed textiles for specific clients, furniture for single projects, and much original wall art. He redrew countless logos and designed a restaurant, parts of a school, modern rooms in a motel, and a gigantic rug for the grand lobby of the Courthouse Square Hotel in Denver, Colorado. In 1946 Girard worked with a coiled spring seating company in Michigan called No-Sag Springs. He convinced the client to let him fully rethink their showroom. His design veered from what they already had, which showed the innards of sofa upholstery (where the springs lived). Girard placed modern furniture in the showroom with intact upholstery. He included chairs by Eero Saarinen and a sofa and side tables he designed himself. *Interiors* wrote, "Springs, even when they don't sag, are not particularly enchanting to look at, decided Mr. Girard, so he simply sat his client's clients on them and gave them something else to look at—potted jungles, fountains, and patios." Girard redesigned the No-Sag Springs logo, including a clever coil on its first "g." His logo was displayed prominently on the showroom sign, delivery trucks, and the company stationery.

In 1950 Girard conceived of a new look for the Fletcher Motel, a humble building abutting a Michigan golf course (see pages 290–91). Using a handful of precise designs, he brought all thirty-two rooms into contemporary style. The motel was a low building with unremarkable details. The rooms had pine ceilings and slim doorways set close together. Girard quickly designed new sofas with unusual upholstery that featured tertiary tones of blue and gray offset by primary red and white stripes. He added wooden Eames chairs and small desks, gooseneck lamps, and slender-legged side tables. Girard then used blocks of color to energize the interior and exterior walls. In some rooms he kept wall surfaces white and painted the ceilings a bold contrasting color. In other rooms Girard put wall color everywhere that pine was not. His couches converted easily into beds at night. *Tourist Court Journal* wrote, "Truly the only similarity between this unit and thousands of other tourist court units we had seen was in the asphalt tile on the floor. From the floor up, the differences were enormous." Girard referred to each room as "just a box," but *Tourist Court Journal* called one room "a Fifth Avenue apartment by day and a beautiful bedroom by night. The charge—a reasonable $6 for two."

In the 1960s Girard created several unique airport lounges, restaurants, and showrooms. He designed two innovative offices in Columbus, Indiana, for the businessman Irwin Miller, whom Girard had worked with before. The first office redesign was for Miller's business, Cummins Engine Co., in 1960. The next, a year later, was for Miller's personal office. Both redesigns were rife with a unique type of opulence—not in the sense of cost or rare materials, but in Girard's arrival at so many elegant solutions. Girard and Miller agreed that both spaces would be restrained. Within that confine, Girard carried on as much rule-breaking as ever. He had gotten a reputation by then for including copious amounts of pattern and color in his interiors. In these offices, he dialed those tendencies back. It was not the only time Girard showed this ability to shift tone completely, but it was among the first times he did so. In Miller's personal office, carpets occasionally moved up onto walls. Secretaries sat in dramatically lit clamshell-like spaces with curved panels. Ample drapes in single colors were affecting and brought to mind large theaters. Room dividers (designed by Girard) pulled down from the ceiling and disappeared discreetly when not in use. All of Girard's flourishes slipped quietly into existence, none saying too much too loudly.

Irwin Miller said of Girard, "To begin with, he is omnivorous ... Next, he is a prophet, and I use this word in the sense of a 'revealer.'" Oddly—or maybe ideally for Girard, who loved contrast—Miller's sleek personal office lived inside an ornate Victorian building. In both Miller offices, Girard channeled many of his ornate tendencies into textures. He created an intricate ceiling out of plaster meringuelike shapes,

P. 256–257 Girard designed and painted the plywood cladding in the Women's Exchange Fair, Michigan, 1939.

P. 259 Additional views of Girard's designs for the Women's Exchange Fair, Michigan, 1939.

← Junior League Little Shop, Grosse Pointe, Michigan, 1938. Top: Storefront. Bottom: Interior featuring a painted mural and winding presentation table.

→ The wooden storage cabinet on the left side of this photo was used to house needlework supplies. Junior League Little Shop, Grosse Pointe, Michigan, 1938.

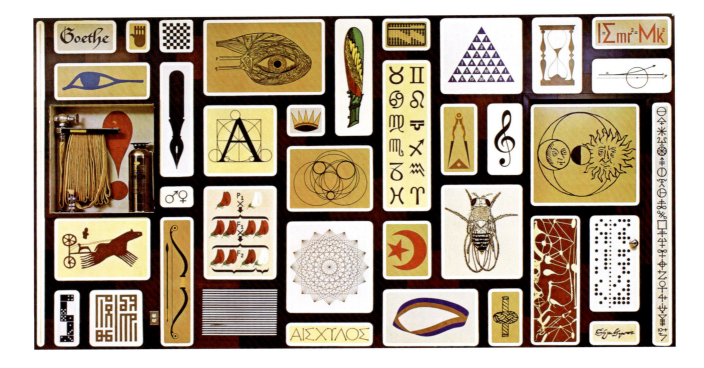

each holding his custom-designed light bulb at its tip. He etched a tiny galaxy of hollows into the thick glass door of a conference room. In the Cummins Engine Co. office Girard mined the theatrics of single colors used in lethal doses (as opposed to his usual symphony of them).

Progressive Architecture wrote of Girard's office designs for Miller, "Several aspects of this work are noticeably different from Girard's other interiors." Interiors wrote, "Almost every detail of the spaces and of their furnishings has been specially designed by Girard, as is his precisionist custom. [He] shows the sublime wit that, at rare intervals, elevates interior design to the level of an art." Girard used pattern only on carpets and window treatments in the Cummins office. One window held ample yards of his Firecracker textile, one of his quietest patterns ever, and one he rarely chose for his own design schemes. Departing further from his norm, Girard did not place a single piece of folk art in either office. He invented quiet novelties in Miller's office, such as a hinged shelf that laid flat against a wall when not needed. He carved orbs from the walls behind doors so each doorknob could float in a perfect void when the door was open. Interiors said it required "acrobatics to achieve such an effect of invisibility."

By 1964 Girard had been living in New Mexico for more than a decade. He had spearheaded a collection of textiles for Herman Miller and designed numerous museum shows as well as two restaurants in New York City. He was having great success working with impressive clients all over the country. Still, the allure of a local job where no travel was required sometimes proved irresistible. Girard's daughter was attending classes at St. John's College in Santa Fe. When the college approached Girard about redesigning some of their interiors, he agreed. He imparted many lovely changes to the St. John's campus. He designed new dining hall furniture, paneling, curtains, and elegant custom lighting that looked like stylish oversized snowflakes. Girard gave several doors at St. John's colorful geometric schemes (more doors than anyone had asked him to address). His color combinations on the doors were unusual and highly customized; not even his grays were from premixed cans of paint. These tones showed Girard's adroitness at successfully (and unexpectedly) combining primary, secondary, and tertiary hues. They also highlighted his gift for mixing bright hues with earthy tones that were rarely seen alongside each other.

At St. John's, Girard designed several striking murals. These were unlike anything he had composed before. The largest mural was an impressive wall of images, each set inside a square or rectangle. The symbols related to one of the seven liberal arts and natural science programs the school offered. Girard placed smaller murals in less central places, such as above two phone booths along a hallway. He said he wanted his designs at the college to be "simple and strong in character." It is unlikely that anyone called his designs simple, but they greatly enhanced the campus. His contributions have been thoughtfully preserved to this day.

In 1965 Girard accepted a second local job, this one at the Unitarian Church in Albuquerque, New Mexico. For this assignment Girard created an impressive and

← Photographic poster of the mural designed by Girard for St. John's College, featuring representations of the seven liberal arts disciplines offered in the St. John's curriculum, Santa Fe, New Mexico, 1964. Girard seamlessly integrated the fire equipment into the mural.

↑ Installed mural in the entrance lobby, St. John's College, Santa Fe, New Mexico, 1964.

unusual back wall lining the pulpit. The wall was composed entirely of small pieces of salvaged wood (five thousand fragments of it). Girard had long been a fan of recycled wood and worked with it when he could. Not long before the church commission, Girard's son was on his way to summer camp in the Jemez Mountains. Along the way he passed a series of old, dilapidated barns, and knowing his father's penchant for weathered wood and his interest in reusing materials that may have been cast aside, he phoned his father to let him know. Girard rarely let an opportunity like this pass him by, and he immediately sought out the owners of the land on which the barns sat to inquire about the possibility of purchasing this wood. Once he connected with the landowners, they offered the wood free of charge in exchange for him doing the disassembly and removal. Girard agreed and, along with his son, showed up to load the wood and drive it back to Santa Fe. Once they had returned to Girard's studio, they set about removing nails, then cutting down the wood into smaller sizes and arranging it by color.

Much of that material went into Girard's Unitarian Church wall. His design was far more difficult to make than a painting would have been, but Girard was profoundly interested in exploring different materials, and weathered wood became a favorite. In crafting the wall, Girard did not use a single drop of paint. Instead he selected wood from the barns and elsewhere that already had old paint on it or a unique weathered finish to it, which created a whole palette to work from; that alone set his illustrations apart from their backgrounds. Girard chose a mixture of symbols—those specifically religious as well as more general archetypes to reflect the liberal and inclusive theology of the Unitarian Church.

This was yet another project that showed Girard's incredible ability to design a project that truly and uniquely fulfilled the client's needs while maintaining his own voice and singular vision. Collage created of weathered wood was something Girard had been exploring throughout his career, and while this was the most monumental example, he would go on to employ this versatile material for the rest of his life, including in the Museum of International Folk Art.

P. 264 St. John's College, Santa Fe, New Mexico, 1964. Top: Elevator wall with solid-colored geometric painted mural. Bottom: 3D model of entire hall sequence.

P. 265 St. John's College, Santa Fe, New Mexico, 1964. Left: Gigantic snowflake-shaped light fixtures with exposed bulbs hang in the cafeteria dining room. Right: Telephone booths with mural and elegant terrazzo ashtray.

Painted doors, St. John's College, Santa Fe, New Mexico, 1964. Girard designed eccentric color combinations for dozens of doors throughout the college.

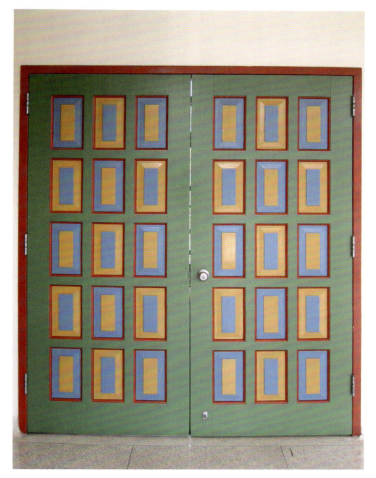

Wooden mural at the Unitarian Church, 30' × 8', Albuquerque, New Mexico, 1965. Girard did not add paint to his jigsawlike mural but used salvaged woods to create inlays for motifs and their surroundings. The symbols celebrate religious iconography and connectivity.

270 COMMERCIAL INTERIORS

← No-Sag Springs, 1946.
Top: No-Sag Springs delivery truck.
Bottom: No-Sag Springs showroom interior. Girard's floating 3D window logo cast sinewy shadows when backlit.

→ No-Sag Springs showroom interior, 1946. Girard decided that no springs would be visible in the No-Sag Springs showroom, only their function.

← Original Victorian exterior of Irwin Miller's office, Columbus, Indiana, 1958. Girard designed the light bulbs and lighting plan for the front entry ceiling.

→ Front desk for Irwin Miller's office, Columbus, Indiana, 1958.

← Conference room, Cummins Engine Co. office, Columbus, Indiana, 1960. For the sweeping curtains, Girard used his energetic textile *Firecracker* in marigold on cotton voile.

→ Two interior views of the Cummins Engine Co. office, Columbus, Indiana, 1960. Girard's longtime client Irwin Miller received an unusual design for his Cummins Engine Co. office, delivering mystery and drama while hiding ordinary office details.

P. 276 Executive dining room, Cummins Engine Co. office, Columbus, Indiana, 1960.

P. 277 Waiting room featuring circular etched glass walls and a ceiling filled with geometric stalactites punctuated by exposed light bulbs. Cummins Engine Co. office, Columbus, Indiana, 1960.

Residential Interiors

ARRIVING IN NEW YORK CITY IN 1932, Girard found it was more common for architecture offices to be closing down than hiring. Given this reality, Girard quickly adapted to the landscape and began working primarily on interiors. Over time he became known for creating new ways to use textiles and new modes to store things, for marrying old architecture with new. His clients loved him and seemingly gave him carte blanche. Girard said, "My greatest enjoyment and satisfaction in the solution of any project is uncovering the latent fantasy and magic in it and convincing my client to join me in this process." Girard got to know his clients well. He designed spaces for them that balanced his innovation and vision with their needs. His interiors often contained bold textiles and always incorporated built-in cabinets and furniture specific to each family. Above all, Girard's residential designs were graceful and functioned well for those living in them.

In creating interiors, he not only designed what he envisioned, but also drew upon his own object collections and his vast network of artists, designers, and makers to bring his ideas to fruition. To most, it was staggering that Girard could deliver multiple pieces of custom furniture to each client as well as custom rugs and lighting. But Girard went even further, creating wall art, custom quilts, new doors his clients hadn't thought to ask for, doorknobs, light switches, faucets. *Progressive Architecture* wrote about Girard, "Not being content to make a collage of available products, he has designed most of the furnishings within the spaces—carpet, screen, doors, wall coverings, draperies, and conference table. He has also reassessed several of the standard details of interiors ... and has given them a fresh and functional interpretation."

P. 278–279 Jackson Lodge, Michigan, 1945.

← Two views of the Feldman family basement, St. Claire, Michigan, 1945. The curved banquette featured pull-down armrests that disappeared into the back when stored.

→ Feldman family basement, St. Claire, Michigan, 1945. Top: A view through the basement, featuring geometric octagonal and rectangular terrazzo tables and a freestanding fireplace. Bottom: The Feldman family basement boasted gorgeous curved slatted wood walls and custom textile curtains.

beds, and clocks. The Hallmark executives were on board for the ride, even when Girard placed an unexpected water fountain in the conference room with a sleek sculpture rising out of it that he had made. Never losing track of his client, Girard created a handsome mural of Hallmark greeting cards along a main wall.

One of the last homes Girard worked on, in 1977, was for Dr. Robert and Peggy Scoren in Woodside, California. It was a less comprehensive project than some of his others, but it was transformative. Because the Scorens were collectors, and because Girard had thought long and hard about ways to display his own collections artfully, he was able to nimbly meet their needs. He designed a unique wall behind the Scorens' bed made of niches outlined in castlelike shapes. Each was well-lit and held a curated group of folk and religious art figurines that Girard had carefully selected for the family. Girard was well practiced in the difficult task of creating a unified feeling from a seemingly disparate group of objects through the expert design of their setting. Having robust conversations with his clients throughout the process allowed each solution to be uniquely suited to the individual or family. The *Los Angeles Times* wrote, "Storage is one of the great needs of our affluent time. Girard has a rare skill that makes that need an asset. He also has a sure command of color and can use it in most provocative and improbable ways." Girard designed a quilt specifically for the Scorens' bed and made curtains using his textile *Palio*. In the hallway he placed fifty of his fabrics on a long wall of cabinets. Girard designed a refined graphic composition from the letters in the Scorens' name that was expertly hand-painted on their front doors, making an undeniably bold entrance to their home.

Textile designer Jack Lenor Larsen said about Girard, "He is Puck—a bright boy with many toys and games to share, magician and fairy godfather. He adds fun to the most matter-of-fact. Always in person, and most often in his work, the humor is as slyly thrown away as a boomerang. Through the corner of his eye he awaits our reaction."

P. 288 Detail of illuminated installation of historic elements from Hallmark's history, Hallmark apartment, Kansas City, Missouri, 1962. Photograph by Charles Eames.

P. 289 Hallmark apartment, Kansas City, Missouri, 1962. Top: Glass-backed étagère wall divider. Bottom: Dining room. Photographs by Charles Eames.

← Exterior of Fletcher Motel, Alpena, Michigan, 1950.

→ Fletcher Motel, Alpena, Michigan, 1950. Top: Room interior with two-tone sofas. Bottom: Room interior with desk chair by Charles Eames.

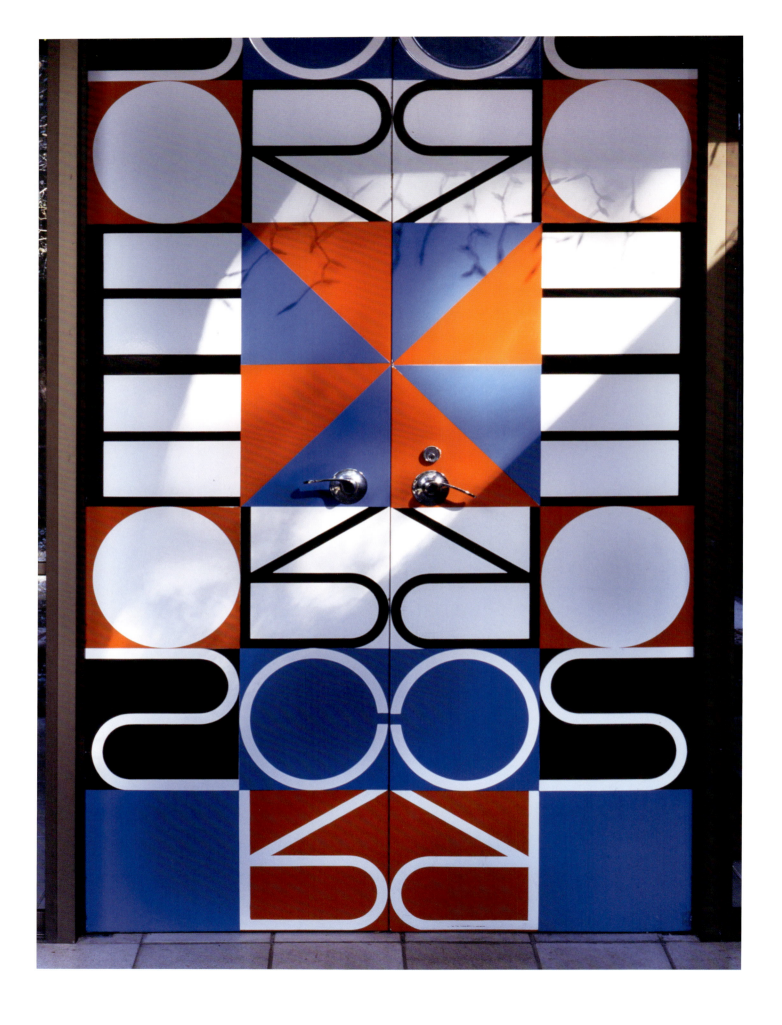

← Enameled steel entry doors, Scoren residence, Woodside, California, 1977.

→ Scoren residence, Woodside, California, 1977. Top: Girard-designed niched wall to display folk art. Bottom: Storage cabinets. Girard used fifty different textiles of his own design on the storage wall that ran throughout the house, employing warm tones for the dining areas and more neutral tones for the kitchen.

The Rieveschl Residence

IN 1951, WHEN ALEXANDER GIRARD WAS living in Grosse Pointe, Michigan, he designed a home for Dr. and Mrs. George Rieveschl that was very near his own (geographically and stylistically). Working as both an architect and interior designer, Girard took on the task of bringing together a number of existing buildings, interiors, and garden spaces. *House and Home* magazine wrote, "This is no hodgepodge, and therein lies the consistency, the art in Girard's work. All these curiously unrelated elements assembled under (and on top of) the same roof look as if they really [do] belong together. This is *collage* architecture. And as in *collage* painting, it is not merely the paste that holds the different bits and pieces together; it is the unifying personality of the designer."

The Rieveschl home included many odd designs. Girard gave the house slanted hallways that tilted up or down (more like indoor ramps) to reflect the property's sloping ground levels. He painted the living room ceiling pink. Doors throughout the home were diversely colored. In his own home, Girard had toyed with some of the motifs he applied here: he had lived with an earlier version of the Rieveschls' partial wall behind the sofa, some radically low-to-the-ground seating, a piecemeal concrete patio, and level changes between rooms. Typically designers experimented radically in private and toned things down for clients. Here all of Girard's designs appeared in more extreme renditions at the Rieveschls'.

P. 294–295 Rieveschl residence, Grosse Pointe, Michigan, 1951. Photograph by Charles Eames.

↑ Girard sitting beside his custom-designed hallway runner that connected the four main rooms of the home. Rieveschl residence, Grosse Pointe, Michigan, 1951. Photograph by Charles Eames.

→ Outdoor dining areas, Rieveschl residence, Grosse Pointe, Michigan, 1951. Photographs by Charles Eames.

← Rieveschl residence, Grosse Pointe, Michigan, 1951. Top: Outdoor walkway paved in salvaged concrete shards. Bottom: Site view. Photographs by Charles Eames.

→ Hallways connect the four main buildings to each other, Rieveschl residence, Grosse Pointe, Michigan, 1951. Photograph by Charles Eames.

← Rieveschl residence, Grosse Pointe, Michigan, 1951. Top: View of the living room showing the stereo built into the sofa. Bottom: Living room cabinetry. Photographs by Charles Eames.

→ Rieveschl residence, Grosse Pointe, Michigan, 1951. Top: Living room, with Girard's hallway runner in situ. Bottom: Living room, with varied elevations shown. Photographs by Charles Eames.

The Rieveschls were a large family with several servants. Dr. Rieveschl was known for having invented the antihistamine beta-dimethylaminoethylbenzhydryl ether hydrochloride, which he renamed Benadryl. Their property had four existing structures, and Girard chose to connect them via narrow transparent passageways. He allotted each structure a new use: one was for kitchen and storage, one for living and dining, one for family bedrooms, and the last for guest and servant accommodations. Girard's layout felt graceful, his choices pleasing—though it was curious why they did. The living room alone had three different floor levels— one the couch sat on, another higher behind the couch, and a third lower in front of the couch on the sunken floor. Girard's plans for the room may have looked frenetic on paper, but in the flesh, the levels harmonized gently. He placed an unusually thick fur on the living room floor (possibly bear) that came up to a person's ankles. A reporter wrote, "Far from completely understanding the house at first glance, you walk around, or on passageways, to hit pavilions that turn out unexpectedly large and elaborate."

As was standard for Girard, he created numerous pieces of custom built-in furniture for the Rieveschl home. He also exposed ceiling structures, designed abstract rugs for their hallways, and installed wallpaper illustrated by the artist Saul Steinberg (a friend of Girard's). He then dreamed up unique gardens and patios around the property. Some had graceful modern overhangs and others looked like appealingly foreign landscapes where concrete chunks grew trees. How Girard convinced the Rieveschls to sign off on so many eccentric ideas is a wonder, but client relations were among the many things he excelled at. Girard had a gentle manner and a wry sense of humor; he dressed conservatively and let his ideas be his most outrageous offering. Over and over clients trusted him. Over and over he infected them with his joy of innovation. Whichever way he gained the Rieveschls' confidence, the result was a sprawling but coherent family compound situated to take full advantage of its beautiful and serene wooded surroundings.

← Living room, with freestanding fireplace, Rieveschl residence, Grosse Pointe, Michigan, 1951. Photograph by Charles Eames.

↑ Exterior at night, Rieveschl residence, Grosse Pointe, Michigan, 1951. Photograph by Charles Eames.

The Miller House and Garden

BETWEEN 1953 AND 1957, ALEXANDER Girard designed the singular interior of a newly built home in Columbus, Indiana, for Irwin and Xenia Miller and their five children. The architect on the project was Girard's friend, famed Modernist Eero Saarinen. The landscape designer was the visionary Dan Kiley. All three designers worked together beautifully, reveling in the freedom their client afforded them. All three contributed virtuosic and innovative ideas (having each achieved a level of mastery in their careers by then). The Miller House and Garden is now widely considered to be a top example of American mid-century design and was preserved after the Millers moved out and designated a historical landmark operated by the Indianapolis Museum of Art. It is a notable stop on historic house and garden tours today. Girard worked separately with Eero Saarinen and Irwin Miller before and after this venture, on a variety of residential and commercial spaces, but for Girard this project became comprehensive beyond compare.

P. 304–305 Eero Saarinen at the piano with Susan Girard, Miller House and Garden, Columbus, Indiana, c. 1953–57. Photograph by Ezra Stoller.

← Dining table with Girard-designed Easter installation, Miller House and Garden, Columbus, Indiana, c. 1953–57. Photograph by Ezra Stoller.

→ Top: Sunken conversation area lined in pillows, Miller House and Garden, Columbus, Indiana, c. 1953–57. Bottom: Xenia Miller's office with patchwork carpet, Miller House and Garden, Columbus, Indiana, c. 1953–57. Photographs by Ezra Stoller.

The Millers were very successful people when Girard met them. Irwin Miller had run more than one large company, most famously the Cummins Engine Co. The couple had a vacation home and owned valuable artwork (a Claude Monet waterlily painting and a Henry Moore sculpture, among others), but they were not set in stone as to what they considered their one definitive style. This was a perfect entry for Girard, as he so appreciated anyone who was open to the new. In fact, it was one of Xenia's stipulations that the interior be able to change to avoid any kind of static feeling. As Girard had already extensively explored this concept of a living interior in past projects and his own homes, he was primed and ready for this assignment. From thorough correspondence and even shopping together, Girard shared with the Millers his methods and philosophies for creating a home that would reflect their interests even as they developed and changed. The Millers were on board, and both trusted Girard implicitly to guide them through this process. One reason Girard could move freely was that Irwin Miller was devoted to forward thinking. Miller had written, "Those who rightly interpret the direction of the changes, and who respond to them, and lead responses to them—such persons in history have mostly flourished. Those who remained the same when the same was no longer fitting—they perished."

The scope of this project was massive and gave Girard another opportunity to employ his skill set of meticulous organization, unique curation, and expert execution. Approaching it all with his architectural training, there were thorough drawings, color guides, inventories, and directions as to how it would all come together. As was standard for him at this point, Girard designed much of the furniture, all of the textiles, and storage to specifically fit the family's possessions. He designed every bit of paneling, every cabinet and rug, and much of the custom lighting. He purchased every bowl, teacup, drinking glass, ladle, cutting board, knife, fork, and spoon. Girard chose ornaments for the Millers' next Christmas tree. He selected new music stands, unique storage boxes, ashtrays, clocks, hairbrushes, shoehorns, soap dishes (and soap, too). What he didn't design himself, he commissioned from his arsenal of talented colleagues, family, and friends, including a number of the whimsical ceramic sculptures, characters, and murals his brother, Tunsi Girard, was creating in Florence.

Girard inserted original, chic flourishes in the Miller house. He created a dining room table made of the same travertine as the floor, which almost seemed to sprout from the surface. He left an open circle in the middle of the table that sometimes acted as a fountain and, at other times, held a solid platform with fake grass or a centerpiece with candles. He devised a unique band, a pretty ring to encircle the center, that had small platforms for folk art, flowers, and more (see page 306). Girard designed customized dinner plates for the Millers for special occasions (as opposed to the plates he purchased for daily use). His own plates had colorful hexagons and charming *M* abstractions that stood for *Miller*. Girard enjoyed turning letters into design motifs, so he also created needlepoint patterns for the Millers' dining room chair seats. Each had a very pretty graphic,

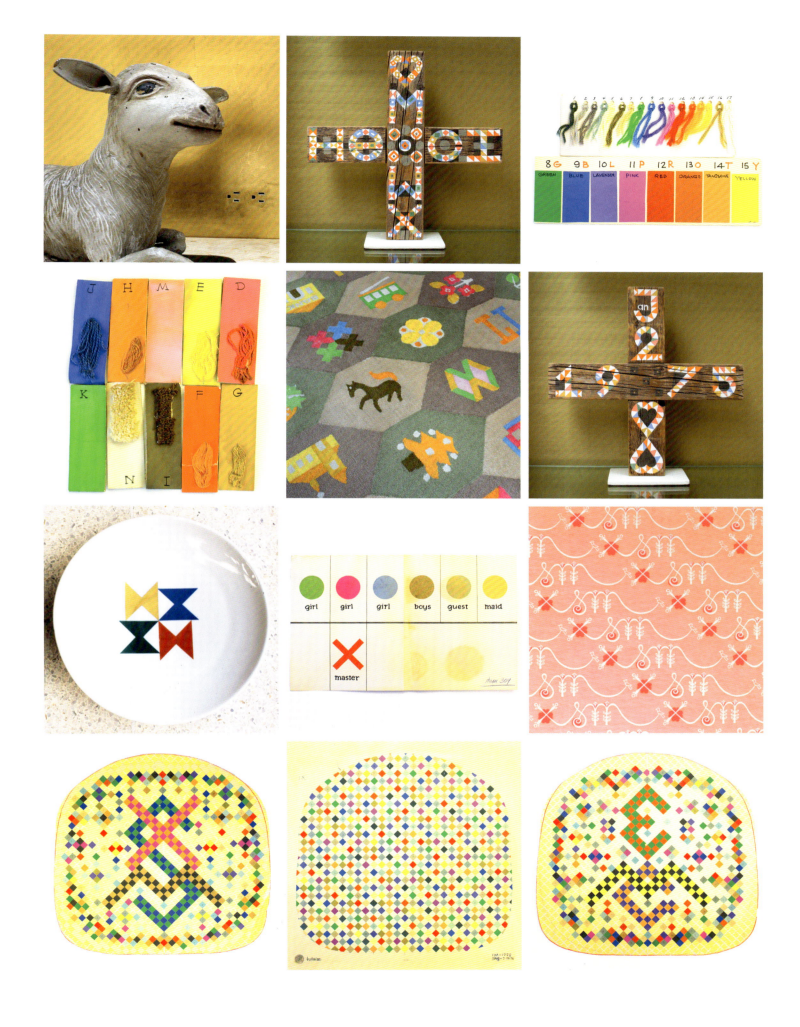

with the initials of one family member incorporated into it (a few extra seats had similar graphics without a monogram, to be used by guests).

Far from being through, Girard performed more acrobatics in the home. He devised a cylindrical fireplace that came down from the ceiling as a sleek tube. It had glass protective panels that opened and closed with the flick of a switch on the wall. Girard also designed customized rugs with symbology woven into their piles that Girard had drawn especially for the Millers—a train graphic that related to Irwin Miller's engine company, a stylized blueprint of the house, and various family initials. Girard focused on many small details: he designed custom napkins for the dining room, stationery for Xenia Miller, and pink tissue paper with her initials on it (for wrapping presents). Girard developed a system for the family's bath linens whereby a dot of embroidered color indicated which bathroom a towel belonged in. He created duplicates for all his textile schemes (pillows, curtains, upholstery) as backups for the family. Not only was this unusual, it was possibly fanatical—but it came in handy for the archived Miller home that is now clad in Girard's original doubles. He was creating a gigantic installation where every single element was part of the whole.

The process between client and designer was collaborative, but the Millers ultimately allowed Girard to play. Saarinen wrote in a letter to Girard, "Then it is Irwin's intention to get on a triangular long-distance hookup (he is now director of Indiana Bell Telephone) and we can discuss the comments. Then he and Zenia [sic] will come to Santa Fe on the 26th and give you a workout on all the requirements." The Millers' "workout" did not dampen Girard's enthusiasm. They approved his fountain design for the middle of their dining table, and Xenia's bridge club agreed to stitch the needlepoint for Girard's chair seat designs. There were a few bumps along the way, such as when the couple had ideas about their fireplace. Saarinen wrote to Girard after meeting with the Millers, "They would like a non-freestanding fireplace—one built into the wall." Who knows what ensued, but Girard's deeply unusual freestanding fireplace is what ended up being built. Saarinen wrote about the fireplace, "I suggested some kind of copper doors or something (common occurrence in Finland). Actually, I think that assuming the fireplace block was worked out as a very rich mural, a fireplace screen would be the simplest and nicest." Girard did not include copper doors or a mural. Maybe he charmed everyone with his captivating custom-designed trunk placed next to the fireplace to hold wood.

P. 308 Miller House and Garden, Columbus, Indiana, c. 1953–57. Top: Painted maquette for tufted wool rug. Bottom: Pillows in the conversation pit in seasonal textiles.

P. 309 Miller House and Garden, Columbus, Indiana, c. 1953–57. Clockwise from top left: Nearly invisible wall plugs, Girard-designed cross with Miller family initials, color test for tufted carpet, back of Girard-designed cross, custom wrapping tissue paper with Xenia Miller's initials, three blueprints for cushions needlepointed by Xenia's bridge club (featuring the Miller family initials) that were made for the Saarinen-designed dining chairs, Miller motif dinner plate, yarn swatches for tufted carpet, tufted carpet with motifs meaningful to the Miller family, color key for embroidered dots that delineated each family member's towels.

← Study with built-in speakers behind lattice folding doors hung with art, Miller House and Garden, Columbus, Indiana, c. 1953–57. Photograph by Ezra Stoller.

→ Dressing room with Girard-designed ottoman with gold-plated legs, Miller House and Garden, Columbus, Indiana, c. 1953–57.

P. 312 Lighting toggles, Miller House and Garden, Columbus, Indiana, c. 1953–57. Photograph by Ezra Stoller.

P. 313 Sitting room with custom carpet featuring motifs meaningful to the Miller family. Miller House and Garden, Columbus, Indiana, c. 1953–57.

Girard lined the trunk in gleaming copper and covered the outside with lovely round discs of wood set flush to the surface. He converted two unmarked rounds at each end into buttons that opened the trunk automatically, like a magic trick.

Girard's sunken conversation pit (see pages 304–305 and 307) was another design he had to sell the Millers on. Saarinen conveyed to Girard, "Zenia [sic] is skeptical about the steps in the living room …Her argument—maintenance and danger with guests falling. My argument—boy! we had a three-story building full of steps—we have eliminated all but three measly steps, etc., etc. I think she will learn to like them—but one never knows." Xenia came around to the idea and Girard installed a fifteen-square-foot conversation pit that was appealing, novel, and comfortable. He developed multiple upholstery schemes for its cushions that would rotate throughout the year. Because the Millers' grand piano was visible from the sunken sofa, Girard had the underside of the piano painted red. Was it a wise move for the instrument's acoustics? It's unclear whether anyone asked.

As a person and as a designer, Girard was tremendously polite and accommodating. He often found stylish ways to give clients what they asked for. This was true of the Millers in many instances. Saarinen wrote to Girard, "In general they would like to be able to close all four views from the living room with curtains for [a] feeling of security at night." Girard placed full curtains on electrically controlled tracks. Saarinen wrote, "They seem to have a certain amount of junk—dead storage is the polite word—in their attic, and we should make possible some storage in the basement for similar stuff." Girard designed basement storage. In addition to meeting his clients' needs, it was also Girard's job to expand their vision and bring new thoughts. He did this handily for the Millers. Girard added many pieces of folk art to their home—select pieces he had collected, and a small number of his own design. He upholstered a sofa in the master bedroom with a shockingly vibrant purple wool (his own textile). In the living room, Girard created a wall of cabinets whose dimensions were sized to the Millers' art books and objects. He lined one with magenta and peach wool felt, to fit their violins. Girard installed outdoor lighting to accentuate specific trees—one toggle illuminated the magnolia trees from Kiley's design scheme, another lit a single oak.

Girard even lent his focus to areas many designers did not usually bother with. In the living room, rather than install standard electrical outlets, Girard customized his by removing their housing and stripping them down to just two simple slits in the wall. In a way he was turning them invisible—until he gold-leafed the wall and made the arrangement unquestionably visible. As in past projects Girard asked the Eames to adapt one of their pieces for this custom situation. He requested that they remove the top tier of their compact sofa design to create a lower profile and apply brass plating to the legs (which would match the brass table of his own design in the conversation pit). He chose gold finishes for the sink drains in Xenia's dressing room bathroom. Luxury was abundant in this house, as was wizardry. In the master bedroom, Girard hid storage shelves behind a wall of artwork (the wall was actually a set of hinged closet doors). He placed stereo speakers cleverly behind mesh wall panels in the living room. As Girard's efforts piled up, they began to collude, to act as multiple parts of a single grand vision. The Miller House and Garden was one Girard idea with many facets. His design was gracious, intricate, and joyful. If visitors were aware that details of the Millers' lives were incorporated into the design, it was exciting. If visitors had no clue, Girard's creation was still a delightful environment they wanted to revisit as soon as possible.

Girard's Studios

DURING HIS MORE THAN FIFTY-YEAR career as an architect, artist, and designer, Alexander Girard's own studios were expertly conceived spaces that could serve multiple purposes at once; drafting tables, libraries, material storage, and an exhibition space all existed together in harmonic function.

Girard thrived having his studio space either in his home, adjacent to it, or not too far away from where he lived. His workspaces were inseparable from his personality; they were perfect embodiments of the way he saw the world and moved through it. These workspaces were in constant flux—he shifted the positions of half walls continually to accommodate each project's needs, redesigned desks and storage structures frequently, and used one studio to showcase a rotation of art exhibitions. In addition to his flexible use of these spaces, Girard's studio designs revealed his unique gift for organizing information without losing the aesthetics of it—evident in his boxes of textile samples that were so attractive they could almost be art objects, and his enchanting drawers full of compartmentalized matchbook covers (a vision to behold).

P. 314–315 Left: Girard studio exterior, Kercheval Place, Grosse Pointe, Michigan, 1940s. Right: Girard studio exterior, Fisher Road, Grosse Pointe, Michigan, 1940s.

← Girard in his Santa Fe studio with prototype chair used for Braniff airport lounges, Santa Fe, New Mexico, 1970s.

Girard's workspaces exemplified the way he used his design skills to lead others to see what he saw. In his Michigan studio on Kercheval Place (designed in the 1940s), he hung a few bamboo window blinds not on windows but in midair to delineate planes that helped establish privacy. Except for a few chairs made by his friend Charles Eames, Girard's studio furnishings were, from floor to ceiling, designed by him. The materials he used for desks, shelving, and walls were mostly inexpensive, but the results were always fetching. In Girard's Santa Fe studio—designed when he was already quite successful and could have afforded more lavish supplies—he made abundant use of humble plywood. This was decades before the material came into vogue. He was enamored with plywood's impossible-to-mimic patterns and textures, and he treated it (and salvaged wood) with the utmost respect. He designed desks, cabinets, and shelving from plywood. He also installed large plywood panels on the walls, as if wallpaper, celebrating the wood's unique striations.

As works in progress, Girard's studios remained current—not to the prevailing styles of the design world but to Girard's tastes, which often predicted industry developments. The use of plywood is only one example of how Girard's offices foreshadowed trends. In his Michigan studio on Kercheval Place, Girard sectioned rooms in unusual ways and erected low walls. He even installed only the idea of a wall (using studs but no sheetrock). Many of these styles were popular a good ten years later. Additionally, outside every office Girard designed, he installed a new sign to keep pace with his latest graphic design notions. The signs consistently spelled out his name but appeared in a variety of treatments and typefaces. Some were freestanding and bold, while others announced themselves subtly and were almost embedded in his front door. No design or typeface was ever repeated.

In Michigan, Girard's 1947 Fisher Road studio functioned as a salon. About once a month he curated art shows with a diverse range of fine art, furniture designs, and folk art. Girard moved in a social circle of esteemed artists, and many of his friends helped make his exhibits special by lending their art or connecting Girard to additional artists. He held shows of drawings by Saul Steinberg and put Charles Eames's furniture on display. Girard frequently showed artists' work that was outside their usual mode or medium: jewelry by Alexander Calder and Harry Bertoia, textiles by Henry Moore, and more than one show of Picasso lithographs. Girard also showcased the work of unknown artisans, exhibiting their folk art ceramics, weavings, and carvings. For each of his events, Girard designed a chic invitation that was unusually petite: a 2¼-inch square. He placed several typefaces on each invite, setting looping round numbers next to hyper-erect letters for the artists' names. The tiny announcements were printed in delectable colors and looked like impossibly pretty train tickets you probably wanted to save. The schedule of shows in Girard's Michigan office space for 1947 was as follows:

January 12—Charles Eames furniture. Lilian Swann Saarinen sculpture and ceramics. Wallace Mitchell abstract paintings. Knoll Associates contemporary furniture. Marianne Strengell woven textiles. Picasso, Rouault, and Matisse prints (sent through courtesy of the Buchholz Gallery).

February 20—A Pan-American exhibit of Peruvian rugs, llama fur rugs, large round trays, pottery bowls, and gourds.

March 16—*Pictures and Things*. Prints, fabrics, and toys for children and children's rooms.

April 10—Work by James Prestini.

May 8—Jewelry by Alexander Calder, Harry Bertoia, and others.

June 8—Modern fabrics by Henry Moore (with Ascher London Ltd.).

September 17—Italian crafts in glass, textiles, marble, wood, straw, and ceramics.

November 13—Boxes and gifts from the U.S., China, Finland, India, Italy, Mexico, Portugal, and Sweden.

The kempt state of each Girard office was a result of him liking to focus on one task at a time. He could somehow do this while not losing sight of the many details in the myriad coexisting projects tucked neatly into drawers and shelves. Assistant Karl Tani said of the Santa Fe office, "It was almost like *House & Garden* was going to come in to photograph his studio because it was so neat. There was just one item on his desk at any one time." Girard's neatness was a trait that not everyone around him could mimic. This was okay with him—he was not strict; he wasn't trying to shut life out. He didn't, for instance, mind when his large dog, Beau, who was afraid of storms, barreled through the office looking for shelter at the first hint of bad weather, knocking over piles of things on tables and shelves.

Interior views of Girard's studio, Kercheval Place, Grosse Pointe, Michigan, 1940s. Girard often outfitted his studios with furniture designed by his friends, including Eero Saarinen and Charles Eames.

In the Santa Fe studio, many of Girard's precise designs were realized by Doc, a master craftsman and carpenter. Doc was very talented, willing, and clever. He was one of the most capable assistants and helped execute many creative explorations. While Girard never had a large number of people working in his studios, he made sure to have a highly capable staff and leaned into their various talents. When Herman Miller sent a New York photographer to take press photographs of Girard's furniture line, Doc and Girard constructed a large light-suffusing tent outside the studio and arranged the furniture inside it. Herman Miller hadn't started making rugs yet, but Girard envisioned a rug for this photograph, so he asked Doc to gather carpet remnants from local shops. Girard selected tan, brown, and black tones, which Doc cut into one-and-a-half-inch strips and then—in the pattern Girard had devised—glued to a large piece of plywood. The result was a handsome fake that looked absolutely convincing.

Girard also had an idea for this photograph to include a clock. He chose a typical desk-sized flip clock but hiked it up onto a four-foot stand to make it work proportionally on the set. To render it unique, Girard tasked Doc with creating an intricate covering; he sent him to the butcher to buy large cow bones. Doc cooked the bones down to make them pliable, then sliced them into very thin strips and flattened them precisely. The strips were sliced into one-inch squares that Doc carefully glued together, making a subtly textured bone mosaic surrounding the clock. The result was intriguing, and Girard was pleased, even though most people might not even notice it. Tani said, "You know, that's the only time that was used, and that clock is, you know, about a quarter of an inch or so on the page [in the published photograph]. But that kind of attention to detail was absolutely incredible."

As time went on, Girard had increasingly more to keep track of in his studios. Work life brought unavoidable accumulation, which Girard had fun with. For the physical matter, he designed delightful, elegant, humorous, and practical storage. Doc constructed many of Girard's customized storage designs, including a set of drawers only an inch high, barely tall enough to accommodate a label (every Girard drawer had a label). Girard designed countless drawers for larger objects, too; he needed ample materials to support his unusually wide range of projects that encompassed interior design, graphics, textiles, and product and display design—performed separately and sometimes simultaneously. Girard's resource materials included differently scaled cutouts of human beings for project mock-ups, drawn or printed examples of interesting fonts, and photographs of books on bookshelves. They also included uniquely carved doorknobs, favorite rubber stamps, multicolored note cards of palindromes,

← Archival storage boxes covered in hand-printed paper in the Girard Foundation, Santa Fe, New Mexico, 1970s.

↑ Detailed views of archival storage boxes with Girard Foundation identification, Santa Fe, New Mexico, 1970s.

Top: Alexander "Sandro" Girard studio logo, 1940s. Bottom: Brass sign on studio door made from reclaimed wood, Santa Fe, New Mexico, 1950s.

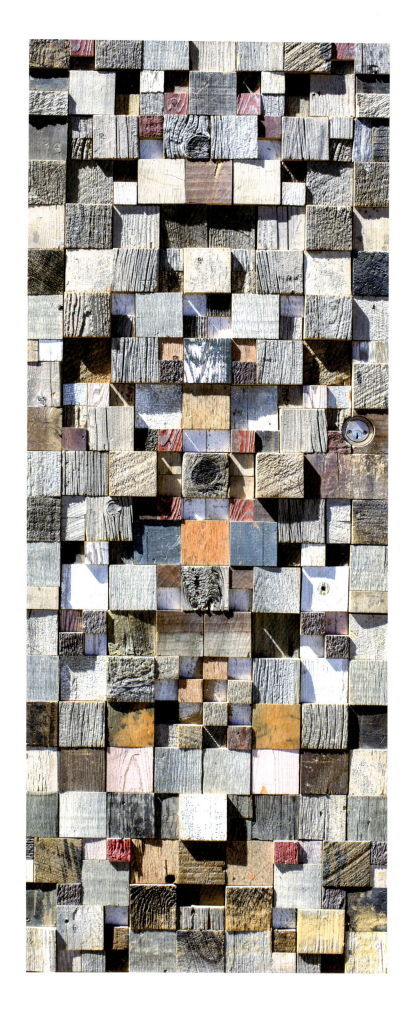

Dimensional studio door made from reclaimed wood, Santa Fe, New Mexico, 1950s.

exhibition 1
october 1 to 11
ESKIMO CRAFTS

exhibition 4
november 20-30
MORAN SPACE SCULPTURE

exhibition 2
october 15 to 29
STEINBERG DRAWINGS

exhibition 3
november 1 to 12
PICASSO LITHOGRAPHS

Invitations to various exhibitions at Girard's studio, Grosse Pointe, Michigan, 1947.

Evolution of the Girard studio logos, 1930s–40s.

paper labels, miniature food, jars of pebbles, Coptic crosses, and typed lists of words that were the same in multiple languages. These were not inconsequential items but were Girard's artist's tools. Alluding to his appetite for things, he once joked that he "specialized in being unspecialized." That was not true; he was very discerning.

At each of his studios, Girard devised specific drawers and files to keep everything accessible. He also designed storage for the growing archive of his own textile and wallpaper collections. He sometimes stored those samples in slim upright boxes and other times in thick cardboard beer boxes his son put together when he helped out at the office, placing small cuttings of each fabric on the outsides, for clarity (see pages 320–21 and 330).

The most epic storage undertaking Girard put his mind to was for his vast collection of what might be one of the most important collections of folk art ever assembled. Girard had been amassing handmade work throughout his career, and his folk art archive came from everywhere on the globe. Girard's assistants interacted with the large store of items at the Santa Fe office quite a lot. Lesly Carr said:

> I don't think he believed in throwing much of anything away ... It's like he had a photographic memory. He could remember specifically and describe perfectly what he wanted you to find. And he would say, "I want the Coptic cross that has this or that," or you know, "the dent over there on it." And you would go through the catalog system. All of the boxes were perfectly labeled, and sometimes it would take several hours because there were—using Coptic crosses as examples—hundreds of them. And so you would climb up on a ladder and pull down a box, and then you'd have to go through and unwrap every single item to try to find which one he was looking for.

In Santa Fe, where Girard's separate workspace was on the same property as his home, his wife, Susan, installed an intercom to call him away from work and make him stop long enough to eat lunch. In order to keep up with the pace of his projects as well as his own innate curiosity and desire to explore ideas, his studios had to run with efficiency. Those who worked for him said it was a pleasant atmosphere, with high expectations for each person to complete their tasks in a timely manner. When Girard believed that you were capable of doing your job, he left you alone to do it. Spending time with his family was also a priority; his studio was a place of organization and productivity, but his children were always welcome if they wanted to join in on a task. Girard worked at tremendous speed at home on many afternoons—so much so that when the staff came in the next morning, they could hardly believe the progress he had made in that impossibly short amount of time. His ability to work consistently and be decisive about each project allowed a prolific amount to get done each day.

P. 327 Girard's hand-drawn stripe studies, Grosse Pointe, Michigan, 1940s.

← Top: Custom wool felt swatches, Grosse Pointe, Michigan, 1940s. Bottom: Lacquer test swatches, Grosse Pointe, Michigan, 1940s.

→ Top: Gloss paint swatches, 1940s. Bottom: Yarn-dyed plaid swatches, 1950s.

← Top: Girard's highly specific studio storage drawers, Grosse Pointe, Michigan, 1940s. Bottom: Beer box textile storage, Santa Fe, 1960s.

→ Inspiration files and collections from the Girard studio, 1940s–50s.

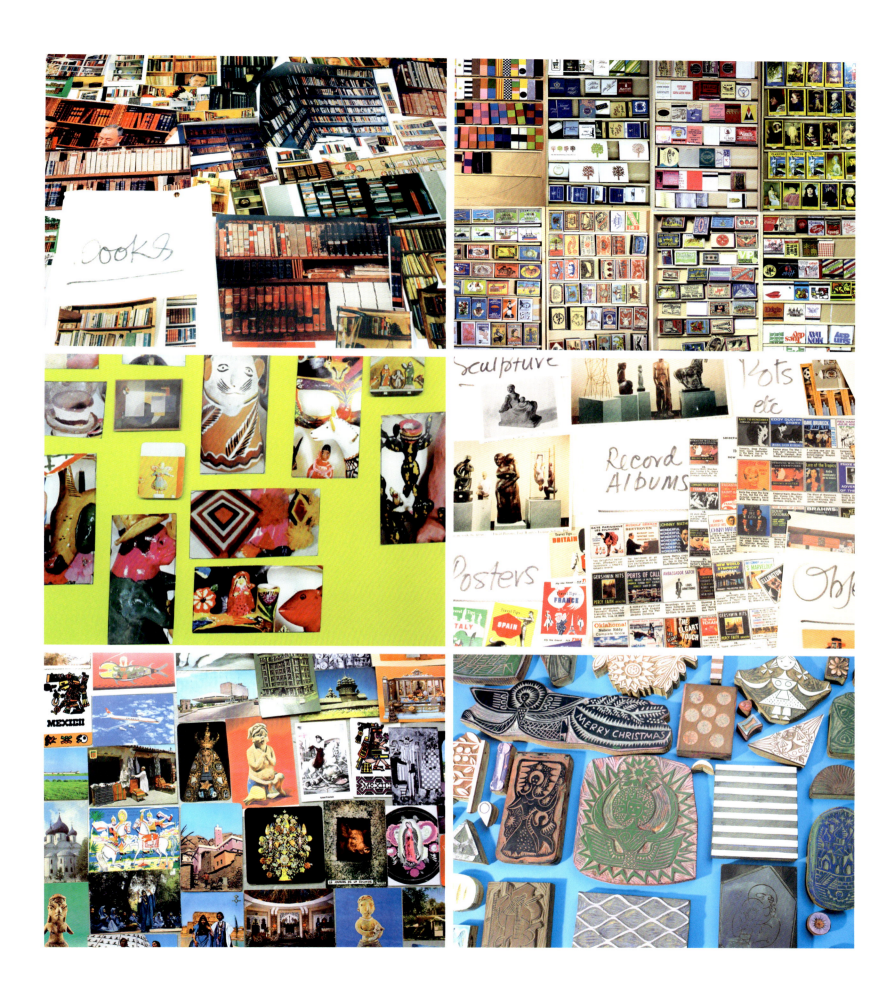

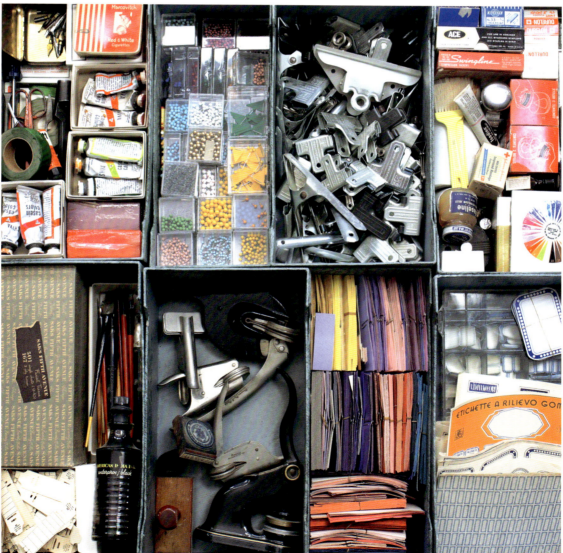

← Girard's Backwards Words Index exploring palindromes and word inversions, Grosse Pointe, Michigan, 1940s.

→ Top: Girard photographed, printed, and cut out groups of people in two scales to include in his 3D models, Grosse Pointe, Michigan, 1940s. Bottom: Details from Girard's studio drawers, featuring art and office supplies (and facial tissue from Saks Fifth Avenue in the lower left).

Girard's Homes

THE HOMES OF ALEXANDER AND SUSAN Girard were constantly changing laboratories of their ideas, needs, collections, and tastes. They had a deep mutual respect for one another, and from that grew a shared aesthetic. Starting with his own bachelor apartment in Florence in the 1930s, then on to New York City, Grosse Pointe, Michigan, and finally Santa Fe, Girard chose to inhabit and renovate existing architecture. He became adept at taking structures with challenging layouts or construction and transforming them into homes that suited the family perfectly. In this way they created a design exchange across time. In their Michigan home on Lakeland Avenue, for example, he changed floor levels between old constructions and new, removed handrails from an older staircase, and exposed ceiling beams. In their second Michigan home, on Lothrop Road, Girard added hallways that connected an existing building to a new one.

P. 334–335 Girard residence, Florence, Italy, 1930.

← Girard residence, Florence, Italy, 1930. Top: Staggered shelf stand and square stools with pieced geometric upholstery. Bottom: Living room with hanging textile panel.

→ Living room with fireplace, custom balcony grate, and sofa with built-in bookcase, Girard residence, Florence, Italy, 1930.

↑ Terrazzo-inlayed tabletop, Alexander Girard residence, New York City, 1935.

→ Alexander Girard residence, New York City, 1935. Top, left: Terrazzo-inlayed tabletop with metal vine wrapping around the base. Top, right: Umbrella sconce with crystal raindrops. Bottom: Curved sofa with reversible cushions (white leather for summer, black mohair for winter).

340 GIRARD'S HOMES

The Girards were flexible when it came to the floorplans of their homes and considered seemingly permanent interior walls as movable to best suit their aesthetic interests at that time. Whenever Girard felt a design concept didn't work, or if one stopped holding his interest, he brought in another. A partial wall of eighty votive candles in his Michigan home on Lothrop Road turned into a folk art display a season later. A panel of hinged wood lattice in front of his bookshelves soon doubled as a gallery wall. An original garage door sometimes acted as a giant living room window, propped open in the summer and fitted with a custom Girard screen. In Santa Fe, in the 1950s, Girard created a conversation enclosure with seats on the floor (it might have been a precursor to the first conversation pit). Then he realized he and his family used it far less frequently than their dog did, and he removed it. He also removed the legs of his dining table in that house for a spate, suspending the surface from ceiling cables. As each concept germinated, expanded, and distilled, his rooms accommodated it. What never varied was the way Girard's best thoughts—those still standing after multiple road tests and refinements—were folded into his commercial projects later, fully polished.

His concept of a living interior that morphed and changed with consistency was in and of itself a reflection of his design philosophy. He said, "As far as I am concerned, the greatest compliment one can receive in this racket is, 'You know, I didn't get a chance to see it properly.' That means there is enough color, detail, and quality to make it almost incomprehensible." To Girard, something alive—even if it was inchoate—was better than something predictable.

Girard's homes offer clues about many of the things that kept his interest over time: He generally placed seating low to the ground, and always had large numbers of throw cushions with interesting upholstery. He experimented continually with wall treatments, sometimes painting them unusual solid colors and other times covering them with abstract or figurative murals or only text. He shifted room levels often, offering his family unique and varied vantage points as they descended into the kitchen or stepped up into the living room. Girard loved candlelight and designed countless vehicles to incorporate it into his homes. He rarely used a freestanding sofa, though he designed a few of his own for Herman Miller. Instead, he preferred built-in seating.

P. 340 Fireplace with carved wooden and glass ornaments, Alexander Girard residence, New York City, 1935.

P. 341 Charming biomorphic forms mingle with silhouettes and type on the walls of the bar room, Alexander Girard residence, New York City, 1935.

P. 342 Sitting room with layers of curtains, Alexander Girard residence, New York City, 1935.

P. 343 Alexander Girard residence, New York City, 1935. Top, left: Pieced striped two-tone carpet in the living room. Top, right: Draped lined entrance to the living room. Bottom, left: Desk with dramatic mirror with carved architectural detailed frame. Bottom, right: Living room with spiraling crystal and brass light fixture.

↑ Stairway with painted mural by Girard's longtime collaborator, artist Bernique Longley, Alexander Girard residence, Lakeland Road, Grosse Point, Michigan, 1944.

→ Entryway with rope banister, Alexander Girard residence, Lakeland Road, Grosse Point, Michigan, 1944.

← Girard-designed kinetic mobile with leaf forms that hovers above a bench with woven blanket cushion and exposed plywood base, Alexander Girard residence, Lakeland Road, Grosse Pointe, Michigan, 1944.

→ Alexander Girard residence, Lakeland Road, Grosse Pointe, Michigan, 1944. Top: Living room entry with sweeping curved wall. Bottom: Dining room.

↑ Sling chair designed and developed by Girard, Alexander Girard residence, Lakeland Road, Grosse Pointe, Michigan, 1944.

→ Bent-wood chair by Girard, Alexander Girard residence, Lakeland Road, Grosse Pointe, Michigan, 1944.

In and around this seating Girard created uniquely sized and situated shelves, nooks, and bins. Examples of these appeared in every room at every one of his addresses. As with his exhibition design, Girard was uniquely concerned with how people moved through his homes. He also added interior windows to create viewpoints into a hallway from the living room, passageways that made you feel you were entering a secret lair, and unusual vantage points for people to take in Susan's immaculate garden.

Girard found imaginative ways to work his collections into his homes. He sometimes came to arrange his objects with as much artistry as the objects themselves possessed. After seeing one of Girard's homes, *Architectural Forum* magazine wrote, "What has become of that old household word uncluttered? The answer is that Alexander Girard has swallowed it, and smiled." Girard had many interior design customers in the 1950s and '60s who also had a lot of possessions and were looking for ways to fit them into the current modern design aesthetic. Girard was influential here and set an example in his own homes.

Each of Alexander Girard's dwellings contained a recognizable flair, even his very first. As an architecture student in Italy, Girard was eager to try out his ideas. Like many young designers with no established reputation, he had to become his first client. In 1929, adapting a studio apartment on the top floor of the building his parents owned in Florence, Girard occupied the space and designed every piece of furniture in it (see pages 334–37). He upholstered every cushion uniquely. He created custom-sized shelves and lovely built-in seating and benches. The *Detroit Free Press* wrote, "The limitations of the funny old rooms fired his imagination … The result was a highly original studio apartment, the first example of modern decoration in Florence."

In 1935 when Alexander Girard moved to New York City, he decorated an Upper East Side apartment with momentous displays of artistry and flourish (see pages 339–43). Girard included many more embellishments than were popular in decor trends at that time. Aware that other designers were sloughing ornate details just as he was celebrating them, Girard wrote, "Functionalism? What is it? Must it mean only the strictly utilitarian; mean unadorned angles, the use of metals in lieu of woods? Must it scorn the curved line? Can it not cover equally well grace and beauty, and richness of design that is aesthetic? I think so … The time is now ripe for a further development beyond this state of austere—though sincere—practicality."

In his New York apartment, Girard hung drapes in multiple hues, designed incredibly intricate wood inlays for tabletops and mantels, and created rugs that were both low and high pile mixed together. There was a lot of decoration in his apartment, a tremendous number of ideas that came together unusually and expressed one charming whole, one very modern sensibility despite its overt ornamentation. Many visitors to the apartment were stunned by the graceful effect of the rooms and by the fact that Girard designed every light fixture himself—every cabinet, rug, and mirror. There was a lot to take in; the sofa in that apartment was upholstered with two textiles—the seat cushions sported leather on one side, to be used in warm months, and mohair on the other side, which was better suited to cooler temperatures.

P. 350 Exterior of reconnected and refurbished building structures that were extended and combined into a single home, Alexander Girard residence, Lothrop Road, Grosse Pointe, Michigan, 1948.

P. 351 Exterior with driveway made from reclaimed concrete shards, Alexander Girard residence, Lothrop Road, Grosse Pointe, Michigan, 1948.

↑ Alexander Girard residence, Lothrop Road, Grosse Pointe, Michigan, 1948. Left: Outdoor dining room. Right: A garage door-like awning opens in warm weather and closes to seal out cold in the winter.

→ Entrance hall, Alexander Girard residence, Lothrop Road, Grosse Pointe, Michigan, 1948.

← Alexander Girard residence, Lothrop Road, Grosse Pointe, Michigan, 1948. Top: Ample and unusual storage abounds in the bathroom. Bottom: Dressing room with glass-front display cabinets filled with folk art.

→ Alexander Girard residence, Lothrop Road, Grosse Pointe, Michigan, 1948. Top: Triangular kitchen counter. Bottom: Den storage and display cabinet.

355

P. 356 Living room view. Girard often redecorated both sides of the angled room divider that separated the living room from the study, Alexander Girard residence, Lothrop Road, Grosse Pointe, Michigan, 1948.

P. 357 Study view of angled wall with artworks hung within the wall's supports, Alexander Girard residence, Lothrop Road, Grosse Pointe, Michigan, 1948.

← Elaborate tiered candle installation, Alexander Girard residence, Lothrop Road, Grosse Pointe, Michigan, 1948.

Girard painted bold colors on ceilings and neutral tones on the walls in this apartment. He created multiple murals, some with text. The more a person looked at his designs, the more his attention to detail came forward. Girard said, "I wanted it to be an impossibility for anyone coming into the room to grasp immediately its full details and the cause of its subtle harmony. I wanted it to have the character that would encourage the study of it. Such a room surely is more restful than an immediate message of what is going on decoratively."

In 1937 Alexander Girard and Susan moved to Grosse Pointe, Michigan. They lived in a small apartment while renovating a home nearby, eventually moving to this residence on Lakeland Avenue in 1944 (see pages 344–49). Four years later, the Girards moved to their second Michigan remodel, this time on Lothrop Road (see pages 350–59). In this home, Girard addressed two older structures by connecting them with a central building. The new volume became his family's common area, and the bedrooms and personal spaces were in the older structures. Girard showed a lot of energetic experimentation in both Michigan homes. He placed textured furnishings alongside spare, modern pieces, finding a unique balance. In his Lakeland Avenue home, he painted a vivid mural on a staircase wall that was not far from a seat upholstered with a South American textile. In the living room, he placed a few elegantly curved plywood chairs that he had designed. These had a lot in common with chairs Charles Eames had designed, and when the two first met, they were shocked at their synchronicity (which bonded the designers permanently).

Girard upholstered and reupholstered sofas frequently in his Michigan homes. He designed numerous storage solutions. He designed a cherry wood dining table that he blithely planned to sand down if it got stained. Everything felt up for grabs; Girard had more room than he had before, and he was eager, agile, and moving at full speed. The outdoor spaces on his Michigan properties were transformed by Girard's innovative use of recycled materials. After a bit of demolition at his Lothrop Road, Michigan address, Girard took the broken bits of leftover concrete and incorporated them into his yard surface, letting grass grow up between their edges. He took blocks of salvaged wood he had accumulated and built a rich outdoor wall surface out of them. It was strikingly beautiful. The collaged wood installation supported a rotating crop of objects that captured Girard's interest (he later created a similar wall in Santa Fe, still toying with its possibilities). Each of Girard's Michigan homes was rife with invention, including a few nascent ideas that arrived from his previous dwellings and got resolved here. Additionally, many new ideas began in Michigan and moved with Girard to his next home to complete their cycles.

The last two of Alexander Girard's residences were in Santa Fe, New Mexico, where he and his family moved in 1953. His first property had two adobe structures that were more than a century old. He joined these together with a new construction and remodeled the older parts. His second Santa Fe home was across the street from his first (this was the property Girard would spend his last years in).

The city of Santa Fe was not yet an art-world destination in the 1950s. Girard said he moved there to have "the luxury of not being interrupted." He absorbed the rich design of Santa Fe and fit it together with his own concepts. His designs evolved quickly, strikingly. A friend of his said, "Having seen the Grosse Pointe house, when I saw the 'new' Girard house in Santa Fe, I was amazed, to say the least, for this was a house built of timber, adobe, brick, and a few stones by the inhabitants of the region. Just what was Girard trying to do? Had he lost his senses? Had I misjudged him, and was he more of an eccentric than the normal person that I supposed? I was momentarily lost." After experiencing the house a bit longer, this friend was won over and wrote this about Girard: "No matter what remote region he visits, he is sure to interpret and give new life to whatever he finds there, on contemporary terms. He is a master at neutralizing the contemporary design trend toward the theoretical and mechanistic, with human warmth and emotion."

Girard designed lovely adobe benches for his Santa Fe homes, and built-in adobe tables and niches. Beams were left exposed. A sleek, modern staircase stood in contrast to the soft clay around it. Where Girard's mantels in New York had been ornate, here they were plain, noble. Girard hadn't left behind his love of ornamentation; he simply redrew it. He painted rich, detailed murals in a number of areas. Two of the larger murals had similar geometric designs and lived on opposite sides of the same wall—one in the dining room and the other outside in the courtyard. The inside mural was painted in cool tones, the outdoor mural in hot, saturated colors. A casual viewer might think Girard tended to adorn his interior spaces in muted colors, but another interior mural, all bright magentas and reds, would prove this theory wrong. Charles Eames said, "Uninhibited by conventional color schemes, designer Alexander Girard has used color in the same unembarrassed way that characterizes his approach to all design in the home."

In the first Santa Fe house, Girard's couch heights dipped lower than usual. He placed some sofa cushions at floor level. Pillows were abundant. Much like he would in his design of the restaurant La Fonda del Sol (possibly as a predecessor to that one), Girard erected a room within a room—

P. 360 Girard installing custom light bulbs in recessed fixtures within white-painted ceiling stripes next to white-painted ceiling vigas, Alexander Girard residence, Santa Fe, New Mexico, 1953.

P. 361 Susan Girard exiting the Girard kitchen with custom wall niches for specific uses such as cigarettes, speakers, and object display alongside a built-in coiled snake clock, Alexander Girard residence, Santa Fe, New Mexico, 1953.

↑ The outdoor dining room in daytime, Alexander Girard residence, Santa Fe, New Mexico, 1953.

→ The outdoor dining room at night with Alexander and Susan Girard, Alexander Girard residence, Santa Fe, New Mexico, 1953.

Living room with built-in benches, Alexander Girard residence, Santa Fe, New Mexico, 1953.

↑ Girard standing behind the cables holding his floating dining table and a wooden cutout Nativity scene, Alexander Girard residence, Santa Fe, New Mexico, 1953. Photograph by Charles Eames.

→ Girard-designed Nativity scene, approx. 36" × 48", painted cutout wooden shapes, Alexander Girard residence, Santa Fe, New Mexico, 1953.

↑ Built-in fireplace on backside of kitchen wall, Alexander Girard residence, Santa Fe, New Mexico, 1953. Photograph by Charles Eames.

→ Built-in niches for a stereo, electrical plug, and a poodle, Alexander Girard residence, Santa Fe, New Mexico, 1953.

which appeared as a large adobe cube—to encompass the kitchen, a unique space where argyles of tiny faux food were built into the cabinet structure beside other remarkable murals made of dried beans or showing measuring standards, bearing paintings of large utensils. Along the outside of the kitchen cube, Girard built niches of different shapes into the wall to accommodate his dog's bed, a television, and a radio. His inventions were a mesmerizing combination of reverence (to the local design history) and playfulness.

In Santa Fe, as elsewhere, Girard designed everything in his sightline—things small and large. He designed and outsourced the making of custom light bulbs for his Santa Fe home, and beautifully intricate brass doors for one storage cabinet. He and Susan designed a garden that they calculated (correctly) would look wondrous when the snow fell. A low brass table from India lived perfectly in the decor of his Santa Fe home, as if it were born there. A snake clock curled very naturally on the wall (see page 361). But nothing remained static, as usual; Girard's decor changed continually. *Vogue* published his first Santa Fe house three times in three years. This speaks of its merit but also its constantly changing guise. As consistent as any of Girard's themes was his proclivity for reinvention.

Notably, Girard's Santa Fe houses were where his folk art collections flooded into his living spaces and took up full residence. He had long collected handmade things: folk art sculptures, paintings, ceramics, candles, and more. In Santa Fe he came up with new ways to display his collections on custom shelves (freestanding and built-in): he placed them on beautiful, customized platforms in delicate niches and nooks. Without allowing his rooms to be overrun, his objects became a bigger part of his environment. Girard said, "The only important consideration is to force things to become part of your life rather than to allow yourself to become, so to speak, a part of things' lives. That's my point of view." In one instance, Girard adapted the usually hidden building motif of studs covered by sheetrock to make shelves. Girard changed their usual measurements to fit his art objects and left the spaces open (without sheetrock) to serve as shelving.

The textile designer Pupul Jayakar said of Girard's first Santa Fe home, "It is a reflection of a very vigorous and vivid mind—a mind that is capable of contracting and expanding—which sees that it's not necessary to find an answer but to be. It is a house that is alive." All of Girard's homes were alive, as were those he designed for others. It was that very essence of life and rejection of a static existence that defined everything he created.

← Outdoor dining room wall with reclaimed wood mural, Alexander Girard residence, Lothrop Road, Grosse Pointe, Michigan, 1948.

→ Alexander Girard residence, Lothrop Road, Grosse Pointe, Michigan, 1948. Top: Drinking kitten in kitchen. Photograph by Charles Eames. Bottom: An elegant Girard table setting.

← Kitchen with painted utensils on cabinet door, sitting beneath painted mural of measuring quantities, Alexander Girard residence, Santa Fe, New Mexico, 1953. Photograph by Charles Eames.

→ Girard used many techniques and materials to adorn his kitchen cabinets. Seen here: illustrations made with legumes, patterned compositions of miniature food, a painting by Bernique Longley, and more, Alexander Girard residence, Santa Fe, New Mexico, 1953. Photographs by Charles Eames.

A rarely seen television in a Girard home, on top of printed linen tablecloth designed by Girard, Alexander Girard residence, Santa Fe, New Mexico, 1953.

← Alexander Girard residence, Santa Fe, New Mexico, 1953. Top: Hallway to courtyard with painted mural. The same mural is painted in a different color palette on the outside wall in the courtyard. A twelve-pointed star cutout of a wooden shutter covers a window. Bottom: Courtyard side of mural with built-in benches.

→ Alexander Girard residence, Santa Fe, New Mexico, 1953. Top: Outdoor mural. Bottom: Gigantic slice of a tree trunk used as a table.

P. 378 Étagère-divided sitting rooms, Alexander Girard residence, Santa Fe, New Mexico, 1953. Photograph by Charles Eames.

P. 379 Girard would often move the vertical wall supports to accommodate the artworks' widths, Alexander Girard residence, Santa Fe, New Mexico, 1953. Photograph by Charles Eames.

← Alexander Girard residence, Santa Fe, New Mexico, 1953. Top: Iron window grate with birds and flowers. Bottom: Scalloped brass table with matching material artifacts such as heating pillows in which a hot coal or piece of wood was placed to create a personal heater. Photograph by Charles Eames.

→ Alexander Girard residence, Santa Fe, New Mexico, 1953. Top: Bench with Checkers upholstery near reclaimed wood table. Bottom: Cable-hung dining table.

← Living room with caramel Eames chair and built-in benches, Alexander Girard residence, Santa Fe, New Mexico, 1953.

→ Tree of life candelabra, with view into hallway of *milagros*-covered doors, Alexander Girard residence, Santa Fe, New Mexico, 1953.

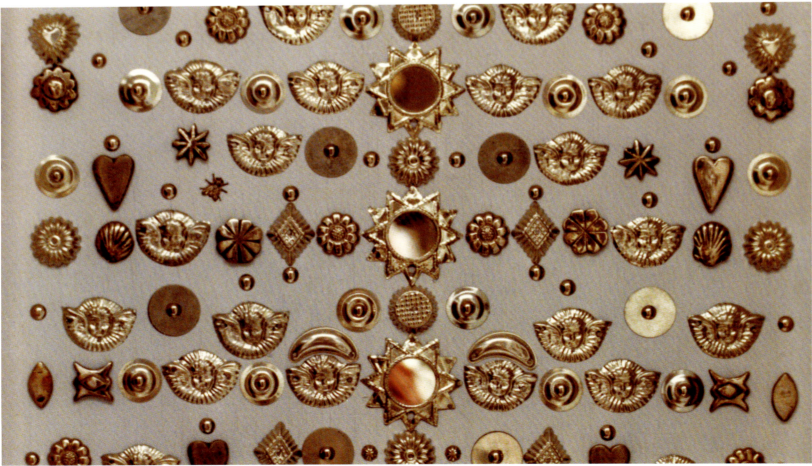

← Alexander Girard residence, Santa Fe, New Mexico, 1953. Top: Girard's collections on display. Bottom: Detail of *milagros*-covered hallway doors.

→ Alexander Girard residence, Santa Fe, New Mexico, 1953. Top: Built-in benches and cabinets in the living room. Bottom: Girard collections on display.

← Two views of Girard's living room, Alexander Girard residence, Santa Fe, New Mexico, 1953.

→ Alexander Girard residence, Santa Fe, New Mexico, 1953. Top: Girard's living room. Bottom: Girard in repose.

Alexander Girard residence, Santa Fe, New Mexico, 1953.
Top: Outdoor living room.
Bottom: Painted tonal wall mural in outside sitting room.

Alexander Girard residence, Santa Fe, New Mexico, 1953. Top: Modern geometric garden rooted in traditional Japanese garden design. Bottom: Alternative view of garden.

Winter in the Girard garden, Alexander Girard residence, Santa Fe, New Mexico, 1953.

391

Timeline

392 TIMELINE

❶ Alexander Hayden Girard is born in New York City on May 24, 1907, to Leslie Cutler and Carlo Matteo Girard.

❷ The Girard family moves to Florence, Italy, in 1909.

❸ Alexander Girard attends school:
Bedford Modern School, Bedford, England, 1917–1924;
Architectural Association School of Architecture, London, England, 1924;
Royal School of Architecture, Rome, Italy, 1931;
New York University, New York City, 1935.

❹ Alexander Girard residence, Florence, Italy, 1929.
Girard's first residential project was the redesign of his own studio apartment located on the top floor of his family's villa in Florence. The elegant studio featured tall folding screens for flexible space and light division, handwoven rugs, and futuristic details such as sofas with built-in book storage and stools with cushions patched into a pattern that today looks pixelated. In addition to Girard's sophisticated, inventive gestures, there were a few accoutrements one would expect to find in a twenty-year-old's bachelor pad, such as a record player and banjo.

❺ Alexander Girard moves to New York City, 1932.

❻ Girard Meets Susan Needham, 1933.
Susan Needham (b. June 1, 1910, in Des Moines, Iowa) was raised in Scarsdale, New York, and attended Mrs. Dow's School for Girls. Her father, Thomas J. Needham, was vice president and director of the United States Rubber Company. Susan was an impeccably organized and proficient student who enjoyed school as well as the social aspects of New York society at that time. She would often accompany her mother into Manhattan on trips to museums, galleries, and restaurants. The Needhams had an interest in travel and took Susan and her brother to Europe as well as on several road trips around the US, including all the way to California. Susan would eventually travel to Florence to attend Collegio Poggio Imperiale, where she would befriend Lezlie "Pezzie" Girard, the sister of her future husband.

❼ Sandro Girard Room, *Permanent Exhibition of Decorative Arts and Crafts*, Rockefeller Center, New York City, 1934.
Girard's wildly intricate installation at Rockefeller Center allowed a sort of turbocharged experiment with details and ideas that emerged in his own house, which he was designing a few blocks away. Girard designed every surface of the apartment-sized installation to the maximum possibility, with relief murals, custom-woven carpets, extravagant bars with burled wood doors, and a wooden crown of hand-carved grapevine clusters.

❽ Girard residence, New York City, 1935
Girard's New York City apartment was a custom-detailed marvel. With seemingly every surface and form considered by Girard, it featured mirrors with carved frames on top of dimensional painted murals, intricate light fixtures of swirling crystals, and crystal raindrop umbrella sconces. Handmade details abounded, including two-tone striped floors, geometric swinging doors in the hallway, and a love letter-themed tabletop, all made from terrazzo.

❾ Girard's modern garden apartment, New York City, 1936.
Arriving one year after Girard completed the design of his New York City apartment, this showcase apartment, also in the city, contained many of the same design explorations, but Girard pushed the ideas further with the pagoda-shaped padded headboards, ghostly tonal plaster reliefs, patterned hand-tufted circular rugs, and bench seating seemingly inspired by African wooden sleeping supports.

❿ Girard marries Susan Needham, 1936.
Alexander and Susan Girard's granddaughter, Aleishall Girard Maxon writes about her grandmother:

> In understanding the vast and varied career of my grandfather, it is clear that he would not have achieved the stunning breadth of what he did without her. Throughout their fifty-seven years together, there was deep and mutual respect, inspiration, and support that flowed between them. My grandfather was highly driven by a desire to make his work but less interested in attaining accolades for it. It was Susan who concerned herself with the logistics of running an office to support

---

1 Alexander Girard carving a block of wood, 1940s.

2 Watercolor done by Alexander Girard during his second year of study at the Architectural Association in London, 1925.

4 Girard residence, Florence, Italy, 1920s.

5 Alexander Girard watercolor painting of the New York City skyline, 1930s.

6 Susan Needham Girard in a field of daisies, 1930s.

7 Room designed by Alexander Girard for the *Permanent Exhibition of Arts and Crafts*, Rockefeller Center, New York City, 1934.

8 Girard residence, New York City, 1935.

9 Girard's modern garden apartment, New York City, 1936.

his many endeavors—managing press for the various projects, overseeing accounting, hosting clients, traveling with him—and governing the household and the children on top of it all. To laud her many accomplishments is not to take away from him but instead to highlight the person he trusted and revered. At a time when a woman's role was typically limited to matters of domesticity, my grandmother stood as an equal next to her husband. Having a keen visual eye, sharp style, and strong opinions of her own, she participated in many ventures beyond the household.

A raw silk dress in emerald green with a thin leather belt defining her trim waistline. Gold bangles adorning wrists and enameled rings on fingers polished with a whisper of pink. Back straight, ankles crossed, cigarette in hand, hair coiffed, lipstick an orangey red, and a powdery fresh scent faintly hanging in the air around her. Elegant, poised, scrupulous, and stylish, she was at ease with herself while maintaining a formality both in her manner and appearance. She was kind and generous while having high expectations of both the environment and the people around her. She had a strong, formal, but loving presence. Propriety was required, but she also managed to leave room for exploration, curiosity, and puerility. This is how I remember my grandmother Susan.

⑪ Charles' a la Pomme Soufflee, New York City, 1937.

This is the first example of Girard's approach to restaurant design. While sparer than a traditional Girard project, it contained many of his classic design ideas, such as the pieced terrazzo striped floors, a bold coffered wooden ceiling, and dimensional plaster relief wall pieces depicting items from the restaurant's menu. Girard's focus on lighting design was in full force with his custom curved and perforated sconces that sent crisp light downward and a mottled light toward the ceiling.

⑫ The Girards move to Grosse Pointe, Michigan, 1937.

⑬ Junior League Little Shop, Grosse Pointe, Michigan, 1938.

Despite arriving early in Girard's career, his designs for the Junior League Little Shop had all of the tenets we often see in his designs. With the curving display vitrines, the elegant Surrealist murals, and monumental exposed storage cabinets for needlecrafts, Girard knew immediately how to organize the space for maximum function and joy.

⑭ Women's Exchange Fair, Michigan, 1939.

Girard turned a temporary exhibition of assorted merchandise into a kaleidoscopic experience by creating enormous wraparound wooden panels painted with his custom typefaces and charming paintings that were for sale. The elegant, all-encompassing graphics hugged the space into a unified experience for the visitors.

⑮ Detrola headquarters, Detroit, Michigan, 1943.

A factory that made World War II communications instruments seems an unlikely assignment for Girard, but his influence on the Detrola Corporation was monumental. Girard started out designing radios and turntables for the newly reinvented Detroit company and quickly set about redesigning everything from the offices, conference rooms, a dining room, and even the production lines of the factory. Girard reconsidered what radios looked like and made them look like sleek, modern objects that at times resembled Susan's handbags. It was at Detrola that Girard met his lifelong friend Charles Eames, then a fellow radio designer.

⑯ Girard residence, 330 Lakeland Avenue, Grosse Pointe, Michigan, 1944.

Girard's experimental home featured a surreal wraparound mural in the stairwell by longtime collaborator, painter Bernique Longley. Girard used his experimental cutout sling chair with fabric support and his bent plywood armless chairs with exposed plywood edges in the cozy living room design.

⑰ Girard befriends Charles and Ray Eames, 1943.

Having first met as designers at Detrola, Girard and Charles Eames became lifelong friends and collaborators, supporting each other's efforts over the years. Despite the

---

10 Susan Needham Girard, 1940s. Photographed by Alexander Girard.

11 Front door of Charles' a la Pomme Soufflee, New York City, 1937.

13 Interior of Junior League Little Shop, Grosse Pointe, Michigan, 1938.

14 Women's Exchange Fair, Michigan, 1939.

15 Alexander Girard's employee badge from Detrola Headquarters, Detroit, Michigan, 1943.

16 Elaborate wooden Christmas tree crafted by Girard in their family residence, Grosse Pointe, Michigan, 1940s.

17 Herman Miller advertisement featuring George Nelson, Charles Eames, and Alexander Girard, 1960s.

18 Sansi Needham Girard, Michigan, 1940s.

19 Interior of No-Sag Springs headquarters, Michigan, 1946.

Institute Torn Apart, Rebuilt for 'Modern Living' Exhibit

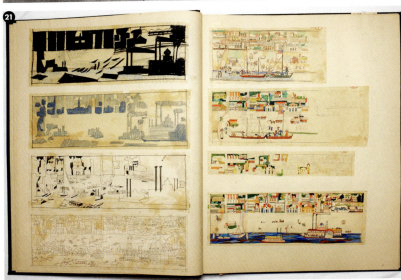

clearly defined design sensibilities between Girard and Charles Eames, it's easy to see their influence on each other. Kismet sculpted a friendship whose influence changed the world of design so profoundly that its effects are still felt today. Their friendship continued until Eames's passing in 1978.

⑱ Sansi Needham Girard is born to Susan and Alexander Girard in 1945.

⑲ No-Sag Springs headquarters, Michigan, 1946.
Girard's curvy furniture designs for the No-Sag Springs seemed to share a form with the company's namesake product. Girard designed the clever swirling logo with its coiled "g," the exterior cladding of delivery trucks, and the main showroom in Michigan, which he designed without any of the company's products visible, showing only their usage in elegant, streamlined furniture.

⑳ Everyday Art Gallery, Walker Art Center, Minneapolis, Minnesota, 1946.
Girard's installation at the progressive Walker Art Center featured roomlike installations of functional modern art pieces alongside his articulated wooden sculptures.

㉑ Girard collaborates with Eero Saarinen for the first time, 1946.
Girard made several projects with Saarinen, including the glorious Miller House and Garden and a few studies prepared for Saarinen's St. Louis Gateway Arch in Missouri. The two also worked together on the North Christian Church in Columbus, Indiana, where Girard designed the priests' and choir's outfits, some pulpit decor, light fixtures, and other interior details.

㉒ Newberry Institute of Art, Boston, Massachusetts, 1947.
Girard's designs for the Newberry Institute of Art in Boston melded utilitarian and exotic materials, such as plywood with shiny lacquers. The project combined fanciful lines— such as flare-legged vitrines with diagonal display faces that eased viewing—with sound ergonomic function.

㉓ Marshall Cutler Girard is born to Susan and Alexander Girard, 1947.

㉔ Girard residence, 220 Lothrop Road, Grosse Pointe, Michigan, 1948.
Girard's wooden-plank-clad residence was filled with daring and unusual design details that added function and flexibility to his home. Inside Girard installed an adjustable room divider, and outdoors, he laid down reclaimed concrete shards, puzzled together with gaps in between pieces to allow grass to grow.

㉕ An Exhibition for Modern Living, Detroit Institute of Arts, Detroit, Michigan, 1949.
The department store J. L. Hudson hired Girard to design their exhibition, An Exhibition for Modern Living, a project that explored new approaches to home living. Installed at the Detroit Institute of Arts, the exhibition saw Girard guide visitors via angled stairs and ramps that connected multilayered display galleries filled with modern treasures— including Eames storage units and George Nelson clocks. Girard created a display hybrid of museum and house design sensibilities that mingled perfectly with his expansive, nearly forest-sized plant installation in the building's interior.

㉖ Fletcher Motel, Alpena, Michigan, 1950.
Motels dotted many American roadways throughout the 1950s; however, it is unlikely that any of them looked quite like the Fletcher Motel. Girard used eccentric color combinations, low-profiled sofas, and bent plywood chairs designed by Charles Eames, alongside expected motel design classics such as matchstick blinds and gooseneck desk lamps to create a cozy experience for those traveling by car.

㉗ The Girards befriend Georgia O'Keeffe, 1954.
The Girards were dear longtime friends of famed artist Georgia O'Keeffe, who lived nearby in Abiquiú, New Mexico. Bonding over their tireless work ethic, a love of New Mexico, and long walks (during which they all collected rocks), O'Keeffe and the Girards spent a great deal of time together, even traveling to Mexico, Morocco, and other locales. When living in Santa Fe, the Girards had a special room in their house always ready to receive O'Keeffe if she came to town and didn't want to make the drive back home. They remained close friends until O'Keeffe's death in 1986.

---

20 Everyday Art Gallery, Minneapolis, Minnesota, 1946.

21 Alexander Girard's sketches of site line studies for the St. Louis, Missouri, Gateway Arch, designed by Eero Saarinen, 1940s.

22 Alexander Girard's elegant desk designs for the Newberry Institute of Art, Boston, Massachusetts, 1947.

23 Marshall Cutler Girard photographed by Alexander Girard in northern New Mexico.

24 Alexander and Susan Girard in their home on Lothrop Road, Grosse Pointe, Michigan, 1948.

25 Newspaper clipping in advance of the opening of An Exhibition for Modern Living, Detroit, Michigan, 1949.

27 Watercolor painting by Georgia O'Keeffe, made for the Museum of International Folk Art, Santa Fe, New Mexico, 1980s.

㉘ Rieveschl residence, Grosse Pointe, Michigan, 1951.

Located a few blocks from one of the Girards' family homes, the Rieveschl residence was a masterpiece of Girard's advanced ability at reimagining space. To create the living spaces, he connected four separate existing buildings through radiating hallways and reassigned each building's usage—the kitchen, bedrooms, and study were all in different buildings. The hallways that allowed passage from one building to another were many, and Girard reprogrammed the experience with vivid custom-woven carpets that looked both modern and ethnic at the same time. The carpet's nonrepeating patterns made traveling within the home a unique visual pleasure.

㉙ Girard creates wallpaper line with Herman Miller, 1952.

Herman Miller launched a collection of wallpaper patterns designed by Girard that were available to the public for more than twelve years. The collections featured many classic Girard patterns, such as stripes and geometric grids alongside village scenes and modern serifed alphabets.

㉚ Girard joins Herman Miller as director of design, 1952.

Girard was made director of design for the textile division at Herman Miller in 1952, joining his friend Charles Eames, who was working there when he arrived. At the time, Herman Miller had an epic roster of talent that also included George Nelson and Isamu Noguchi. Girard made hundreds of textiles, furniture designs, and more throughout his twenty-one-year career with Herman Miller. Many of Girard's original designs are still in production today.

㉛ Girard residence, Santa Fe, New Mexico, 1953.

Girard's family house in Santa Fe was in a constant state of evolution and experimentation, with many explorations showing up in his design projects. The level of fine-tuning and detail throughout the house was staggering and perfectly personal, containing all and only what Girard loved most.

㉜ *Good Design*, Chicago, Illinois, Merchandise Mart, 1953, and New York City, Museum of Modern Art, 1954.

Good Design was an ongoing and ever-changing exhibition that was installed in the Chicago Merchandise Mart and the Museum of Modern Art in New York City. The show was a multilayered installation of housewares and designs displayed on Girard's long floating glass shelving.

㉝ Miller House and Garden, Columbus, Indiana, 1953.

The Miller House and Garden is an astonishing monument to mid-century design. Working together with Eero Saarinen, Girard was listed as both an architect and interior designer on this magnificent project, which also included Dan Kiley as head of landscape design. In taking on this job, Girard's consideration of the Miller family's needs was profound and immaculately delivered. It is full of extraordinarily laborious design details as well as the site of one of the first recessed seating areas, which came to be known as a conversation pit. This project is an excellent example of Girard's incredible ability to both communicate with his clients and intuit their needs. From a custom-designed rug with symbols to represent the family to personal gift-wrapping paper featuring Xenia Miller's initials, Girard considered the smallest of details. The Miller House and Garden is maintained by the Indianapolis Museum of Art as the repository of record for the project and can be toured by appointment. The house contains almost all of the original details, and its design feels as fresh today as it did upon completion in 1953.

㉞ Girard creates table settings for Georg Jensen, New York City, 1955.

Girard was asked to design modern dinnerware for the sophisticated tabletop design company Georg Jensen in New York City. A year after the collection's debut, Girard designed elaborate tabletop tableaus with name plates fashioned from wine corks, construction paper, and plaster jelly molds. On the back of the invitation to the opening night party in April 1956, Girard wrote, "This Exhibition of table settings came to be because Jensen's asked me to express my own and my wife's predilection for the

---

27 Watercolor painting by Georgia O'Keeffe, made for the Museum of International Folk Art, Santa Fe, New Mexico, 1980s.

28 Outdoor dining at the Rieveschl residence, Grosse Pointe, Michigan, 1951.

29 Announcement for Alexander Girard wallpaper collection for Herman Miller, 1952.

30 Top: Charles Eames, Alexander Girard, and George Nelson, featured in *Grand Rapids Market Daily News*, 1950s. Bottom: Actress Lauren Bacall wearing pants made from Alexander Girard's wool check textile designed for Herman Miller, 1950s.

31 Alexander Girard in Santa Fe, New Mexico, 1950s.

33 Alexander Girard's pencil sketch for dining table decor in the Miller House and Garden, Columbus, Indiana, 1953.

34 Tablecloth drawing by Alexander Girard for Georg Jensen, New York City, 1955.

35 Alexander Girard's pencil drawing for a gigantic hand tufted rug for Courthouse Square Hotel, Denver, Colorado, 1958.

· herman · miller · ·
announces · a · new ·
· · collection · of ·
40 · hand · printed ·
· wallpapers · by · ·
alexander · girard
and · coordinated ·
· with · the · herman
· miller · fabrics ·
fabric - wallpaper
· sample · book · $10
papers · only · $2.50
· on · view · in · new ·
york · chicago · los
angeles · & · grand

THREE FAMOUS HEADS GET TOGETHER — Herman Miller Furniture Co.'s three outstanding designers take a breather from Market activity. Left to right are Charles Eames, Alexander Girard and George Nelson.

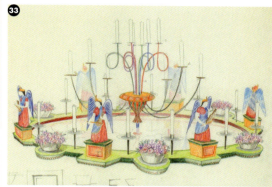

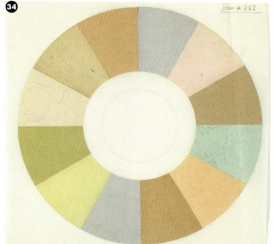

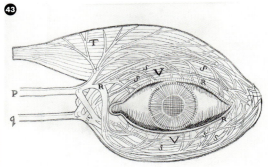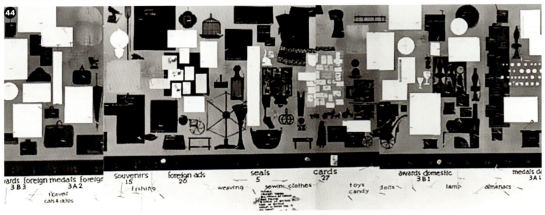

enjoyment of all of the many small things that come into our everyday lives. It was not our intention to revolutionize the food we eat or how we eat it, but rather to emphasize some of the things useful, playful, or ceremonial that can create pervading moods at mealtimes."

㉟ Courthouse Square Hotel, Denver, Colorado, 1958.

Girard was among several contributing designers and architects who worked on this project, including I. M. Pei. In addition to his textile designs used throughout the hotel, Girard created a tremendously large custom rug for the lobby as well as a color-coordinated rug for the mezzanine.

㊱ Cummins Engine Co. office, Columbus, Indiana, 1960.

The Cummins Engine Co. office was the first of two offices Girard designed for Irwin Miller's family business. It was a conspicuously spare design for Girard that removed any clues of the office's activity and replaced it with giant swaths of curtains, carpet, and filing cabinets in muted jewel tones that glowed in dramatic recessed lighting.

㊲ La Fonda del Sol, New York City, 1960.

At the recommendation of architect Philip Johnson, Girard was hired to create New York City's first Latin American restaurant, La Fonda del Sol. The volume of objects, interior design details, and graphic designs Girard created for this project rivals the number he would prepare for Braniff International Airways in 1965. Girard shaped the challenging shotgunlike floor plan of the building into multiple private dining rooms that made each visit to the restaurant a unique experience. From the hand-painted ceramic sun-shaped hot water faucet knobs in the bathrooms to the custom-shaped shot glasses labeled *Tequila*, it is hard to identify anything at La Fonda del Sol that Girard didn't design and make (except for the chairs, which were designed by Charles Eames, though Girard requested a special version made with lower backs).

㊳ Textiles & Objects Shop, New York City, 1961.

Girard designed the charming retail shop Textiles and Objects (T&O) for Herman Miller. Located on East 53rd Street in New York City, it was stocked exclusively with objects and textiles designed or curated by Girard and was the first time that folk art was seen at a retail location in New York. For the shop, Girard made mirrors using patchworked textiles as well as pillows from his many textile collections, grouping nonmatching pillows alongside his crisp lined textiles. Girard reimagined the long, narrow store's footprint into several showroomlike experiences divided by lighted étagères and sheer fabric panels that encouraged visitors to explore the next room.

㊴ Miller office, Columbus, Indiana, 1961.

Girard was proving to be a master at integrating his modern design sensibilities with whatever building form he encountered, and the Victorian building of Irwin Miller's office was no different. Girard mingled rectangular exposed light bulb clusters in the ornate entry coffers with a front desk so sleek it hid any signs of the office's operation. This was the second office Girard designed for Irwin Miller.

㊵ Hallmark apartment, Kansas City, Missouri, 1962.

The Hallmark company commissioned Girard to reimagine its ten-room corporate guest apartment in Kansas City. Girard designed a museum-like installation of Hallmark ephemera alongside opulent tables made of malachite and an indoor pond filled with plants that sprouted a futuristic square fountain. For each bedroom, he designed built-in entertainment centers with a recessed television, stereo, and clock.

㊶ Creation of the Girard Foundation, 1962

Girard formally created a foundation to protect and organize his museum-sized collection of treasures, including handicrafts, toys, posters, religious iconography, and exquisite oddities from all over the world. His generous gift of thousands of pieces of folk art from the foundation to the Museum of International Folk Art in Santa Fe, New Mexico, created the entirety of the Girard wing's installations still on display today.

㊷ *The Nativity*, Nelson Gallery, Kansas City, Missouri, 1962.

Curated from the Girard Foundation's collection, the 150 crèches Girard chose for this exhibition represented many different artistic techniques, aesthetics, and materials, including one ceramic crèche created by his talented brother, Tunsi Girard.

---

36 Meeting room at the Cummins Engine Co. office, Columbus, Indiana, 1960.

37 Alexander Girard-designed hot water faucet at La Fonda del Sol, New York City, 1960.

38 Top: Exterior of T&O storefront, New York City, 1961. Bottom: Alexander Girard-designed woven silk ties sold at T&O, 1961.

39 Front reception desk, Miller office, Columbus, Indiana, 1961.

40 Built-in entertainment center for Hallmark apartment, Kansas City, Missouri, 1962.

41 Paper-covered archival boxes from the Girard Foundation, 1962.

42 Nativity tableau from the Girard Foundation, 1962.

43 Drawing for the entry hall mural for St. John's College, Santa Fe, New Mexico, 1964.

44 Top: Girard installing John Deere mural, Moline, Illinois, 1964. Bottom: Sketch for John Deere installation, 1962.

㊸ St. John's College, Santa Fe, New Mexico, 1964.
St. John's College is unusual in that it was more of a redesign than Girard's usual design takeover. He added eccentric, vibrant color combinations in geometric volumes, clean-lined designs, and scientific murals that are still in place today. To prepare the mural that greets students as they enter the school, Girard hand-drew full-scale images from each of the seven learning tenets explored at St. John's. The gigantic snowflakelike light fixtures he designed for the student dining room still twinkle above the long dining tables today. More than a dozen color palettes were prepared to paint the hand-carved doors that Girard then sequenced in a beguiling, non-repeating layout.

㊹ John Deere, Moline, Illinois, 1962–1964.
Preparations for the monumentally scaled mural installation that Girard placed in the John Deere corporate office in Moline, Illinois, went on for several years. The Girards combed through thrift stores and flea markets around the midwest, on the hunt for Americana objects to help describe John Deere's history, creating an installation with more than two thousand pieces. Several John Deere employees shared stories of Girard finding jewels from John Deere history right in their offices and "borrowing" them for his permanent installation.

㊺ Unitarian Church mural, Albuquerque, New Mexico, 1965.
Girard sourced all the wood for this mural from his enormous cache of reclaimed wood. Working with the faded colors of the recycled wood, Girard assembled the collage by cutting the planks into small squares that he then inlaid to create the larger composition of religious and spiritual symbols. This project is still intact today.

㊻ Braniff International Airways, Dallas, Texas, 1965.
Girard prepared an astonishing number of designs for the Dallas-based Braniff International Airways. Flying with Braniff became, in Girard's hands, a joyful pleasure at every turn. His clever textile combinations referenced Latin American handcrafts and Braniff destinations. When mixed with his crisp, spare graphics and folk art collection, there resulted a thrilling paradox. Braniff continued using Girard's designs for years, but even Girard could not have imagined the beguiling addition that came to appear next to his airport lounge designs after Braniff began building its new terminal location at Dallas Fort Worth Airport and discovered a seventy-million-year-old, ten-thousand-pound plesiosaur fossil, which the airline company reassembled and installed between gates ten and eleven.

㊼ L'Etoile, New York City, 1966.
Having just executed his extravagant Braniff project, Girard took a sharp turn in both color choices and experience. L'Etoile restaurant existed on multiple floors, providing a more private or specific experience to its guests. Its French inspirations ranged from the names of writing luminaries etched in glass panels and its patriotic red, white, and blue upholstery. On an upper floor, the walls of a dining room had a more recognizable Girard approach as they were lined with his panels of mixed geometric textiles. At the same time Girard was designing L'Etoile, he was working on the Compound restaurant in Santa Fe, New Mexico.

㊽ The Compound, Santa Fe, New Mexico, 1966.
The James Beard award-winning restaurant the Compound is the only Girard restaurant project that is still operating with most of its original design intact. Inspired by its southwestern location and the 250-year-old adobe building in which it is housed, Girard created a fusion of hyper-clean lines and bold hand-hewn materials such as the brass and steel moon and sun and a ceiling created from a patchwork of antique Navajo rugs. Girard designed and hand-painted wooden cutouts that he installed in the niches and on walls, placing clusters of folk art in altar-shaped glass-front wall vitrines alongside them.

㊾ Girard Group for Herman Miller, 1967.
After designing furniture for individual projects for years, Girard released his first commercially available collection of furniture with Herman Miller. The collection consisted of perfectly coordinated yet not matching sofas, chairs, ottomans, and tables. The low-profile seat heights were unusual for the day, sending the user into an instantly relaxed position. The plentiful upholstery choices proved daunting for customers, requiring selections from hundreds of color options for upper and lower sofa areas, seats, and cushion welting.

---

45 Girard's signature in the wooden construction for the Unitarian Church in Albuquerque, New Mexico, 1965.

46 Top: Exterior paint schemes for Braniff International Airways, Dallas, Texas, 1965. Bottom: Andy Warhol and Sonny Liston in an advertisement for Braniff International Airways, 1960s.

47 Left: Matchbook drawing for L'Etoile restaurant. Right: Actor Mia Farrow against a tile-and-mirror-clad wall in L'Etoile, 1966.

48 Metal sign for the Compound restaurant, Santa Fe, New Mexico, 1966.

49 Cover of a catalog introducing the Girard Group furniture collection, 1967.

50 Elaborate installation at The Magic of a People, San Antonio, Texas, 1968.

(50) *The Magic of a People,* HemisFair '68, San Antonio, Texas, 1968.
For the World's Fair held in 1968 in San Antonio, Texas, Girard designed and curated an epic experience titled *El Encanto de un Pueblo (The Magic of a People).* In usual fashion, every aspect of the project was considered, even keeping the visitors engaged while they waited in line outside with bossy angels offering instructions, tree of life murals, and elegant multi-hued painted panels alongside the ramps that welcomed guests in. Girard's paint scheme for the exterior changed as it met a corner, creating giant planes of color that felt as light as air and without visual depth. The color organization was guided by sunrise pinks, oranges, and yellows near the charming brass sun inlaid on the face of the exhibition that transitioned into blue shades behind the silver inlaid moon and stars. Once inside, Girard presented visitors with a complex and wildly intricate tableaux of city, village, and mountain scenes filled with folk art families that included more than five thousand pieces of American and South American folk art.

(51) Girard's grandchildren are born.
Mario Cutler Girard (b. 1969), Alexander Kori Girard (b. 1979), Molly Coonan (b. 1980), and Aleishall Daisy Karen Girard (b. 1981).

(52) Environmental Enrichment Panels for Herman Miller, 1971.
Girard's very large, printed panels were created as a sort of visual antidote to the cold and impersonal designs behind the cubicle workplace system Action Office. Girard drew full-scale versions of many of his beloved motifs, such as suns, stars, and geometric patterns, printing them all in one color (except *Triple Eyes,* made with three colors and featured on this book's cover, as well as *Girls*) that were ultimately mounted on walls and ceilings of these offices, waking up and infusing much-needed personality into the austere, impersonal spaces. All but one of the panels was printed on textured, solid-colored fabrics made in Mexico called *Mexicotton.* The lone anomaly, *Bouquet,* was printed on a cheery mixed-stripe background.

(53) Scoren residence, Woodside, California, 1977.
Among the last of Girard's residential projects, the Scoren residence in California featured a front door with sinewy enameled type designed by Girard, a bedroom with sky blue outlined niches for folk art, and curtains made of the 1964 textile *Palio.* An extraordinary fifty-door storage cabinet/room divider featured doors clad in Girard's custom-designed textiles, which he also pieced into a quilted bedspread.

(54) *Multiple Visions: A Common Bond,* Museum of International Folk Art, Santa Fe, New Mexico, 1981.
Girard's last exhibition design at the Museum of International Folk Art in Santa Fe, New Mexico, was certainly his most personal. The herculean exhibition, consisting of thousands of pieces of folk art from more than one hundred countries, was made entirely from Girard's enormous gift of his folk art collection to the museum. Girard designed, placed, and curated each display, depicting situations from everyday life. Girard donated 106,000 toys, dolls, paintings, pieces of beadwork, pieces of religious folk art, masks, textiles, sugar skulls, and Japanese robots to the museum. Despite the magnitude of Girard's curation of more than 13,000 objects that make up the astonishing permanent exhibition, the balance of the collection—over one hundred thousand pieces—are stored and protected in the museum's archive.

(55) Alexander Hayden Girard passes away in Santa Fe, New Mexico, December 31, 1993.

(56) Susan Winifred Josephine Needham Girard passes away, Santa Fe, New Mexico, February 1, 1996.

(57) The Girard Foundation dissolves, 1996.
Girard's careful preservation of his work over the years created a volume of design treasures so large it proved difficult to find the right institution to house and preserve it. Eventually it became clear that the European design collective Vitra could support the collection, alongside other iconic collections, including those of Charles and Ray Eames, George Nelson, Verner Panton, and Harry Bertoia.

(58) Girard Studio opens, Berkeley, California, 2012.
The Girard family created Girard Studio to promote and preserve the extraordinary legacy of Alexander Girard. The studio operates as the official representation of this profound body of work.

51 Left: Georgia O'Keeffe, Susan and Alexander Girard with their grandchild Mario. Right: Alexander Girard and his grandchildren Aleishall, Molly, and Kori, 1980s.

52 *Circle Sections,* Environmental Enrichment Panel, 1971.

53 Fabric-covered cabinets at the Scoren residence, Woodside, California, 1977.

54 Folk art stored in the archive of the Museum of International Folk Art, Santa Fe, New Mexico.

57 Susan and Alexander Girard in the Girard Foundation, 1980s.

58 Alexander Kori Girard and Aleishall Girard Maxon work to preserve and share the Girard legacy.

Index

Action Office, 132, 142, 405
alphabets. See graphic design; typefaces
architecture fused with interior design, 13, 278, 294

Beard, James, 402
Bertoia, Harry, 317, 405
Braniff International Airways, 85, 106, 148–53, 148–65, 210, 316, 401, 402, 403

Café Trouville, 222, 256
Calder, Alexander, 317
Charles' a la Pomme Soufflee, 222, 228, 228–29, 256, 394, 395
Chicago Merchandise Mart, 178, 398
cityscape color scheme (Columbus, IN), 17, 18
collages, 35, 44, 46, 48, 58, 61, 94, 98, 118, 176, 180, 232, 265, 278, 294, 402, 403
commercial interiors, 256–65, 256–77. See also specific enterprises
Compound restaurant, 210, 216, 222, 228–32, 232–35, 402, 403
Courthouse Square Hotel, 258, 399, 401
Cummins Engine Co., 17, 68, 258–62, 274–77, 308, 400, 401

Detroit Institute of Arts, 17, 178, 396, 397
Detrola Corporation, 10, 13, 45, 166–69, 166–75, 179, 181, 228, 394, 395

Eames, Charles, 13, 36, 39, 45, 106, 124, 151, 166, 312, 317, 360–61, 394–98, 395, 405
  chairs, 152, 163, 184, 246, 252–53, 255, 258, 288, 290, 291, 317, 318, 360, 382, 401
Eames, Ray, 13, 36, 39, 106, 312, 394, 405
Environmental Enrichment Panels, 53, 132–42, 132–41, 213, 405
  Black and White, 132, 141
  Bouquet, 53, 140, 405
  Circle Sections, 404
  Crosses, 139
  Daisy Face, 138
  Geometric, 139
  Girls, 135, 405
  Hand and Dove, 132, 136
  Leaf Clover, 138
  Love Hearts, 132, 137, 232
  New Sun, 53, 136
  Old Sun, 138
  Palace, 139
  Paper Dolls, 132, 136
  Triple Eyes, 138, 405
Everyday Art Gallery, 178, 179, 181–83, 396, 397
exhibition design, 17, 176–207, 176–207. See also specific museums

Feldman family basement, 280–82, 288

Fletcher Motel, 258, 290–91, 397
folk art, 12, 115–16, 121, 132, 151, 153, 164, 178, 180, 184, 187–207, 188–96, 206–7, 236, 262, 290, 293, 306, 312, 317, 326, 331, 342, 354, 370, 378–79, 400, 401–402, 403–4, 405
furniture. See product design

Georg Jensen, 106, 142–43, 142–47, 398–401, 399
Gernreich, Rudi, 248, 255
Girard, Alexander Hayden ("Sandro")
  biographical facts and family members, 8, 10, 13, 17, 42, 100, 176, 194–95, 197, 262, 278, 326, 334, 350, 360–61, 393–405
  homes of. See Girard's residences
  languages, mastery of, 195, 208, 255
  nickname ("Mouse"), 232
  personality of, 121, 180, 197, 290, 302, 312, 314, 317, 320, 326
  pet dogs and cats, 26, 37, 41, 317, 320, 342, 369, 370, 371
  photographs by, 38, 86, 91, 115, 395–96
  photographs of, 7–10, 36–37, 39, 41, 55, 59, 123, 132, 146, 174, 178, 194, 199, 296, 316, 360, 363, 366, 387, 392, 395–96, 399–400, 404
  studios of. See Girard's studios
  timeline, 392–405
  travels of, 98, 180, 194–95, 197, 236, 397
Girard, Marshall Cutler (son), 37, 216, 265, 396, 397
Girard, Sansi Needham (daughter), 37, 262, 395, 397
Girard, Susan Winifred Josephine Needham (wife), 8, 10, 13, 176, 258, 326, 360, 393–94, 397, 405
  gardens of, 350, 370, 389–91
  photographs of, 36–37, 39, 55, 114, 146, 199, 305, 361, 363, 392, 395–96, 404
  travels of, 180, 195
Girard Foundation, 197, 199, 320–21, 400, 401, 404, 405
Girard Furniture Collection, 100, 100–103
Girard Group for Herman Miller, 85, 106, 107–11, 402, 403
Girard's residences, 334–70, 334–91
  Florence, Italy, 194, 334, 334–37, 350, 392, 393
  Lakeland Road, Grosse Pointe, MI, 334, 344–49, 360, 394, 395
  Lothrop Road, Grosse Pointe, MI, 7, 13, 334, 342, 350–59, 360, 370–71, 396, 397
  NYC apartments, 194, 334, 338–43, 350, 360, 392, 393
  Santa Fe, NM, 13, 17, 197, 326, 334, 342, 360–61, 360–69, 370, 372–91, 397, 398
Girard Studio (Berkeley), 405
Girard's studios, 8–9, 10, 314–26, 314–33
  Fisher Road, Grosse Pointe, 315, 317
  invitations to exhibitions, 317, 324
  Kercheval Place, Grosse Pointe, 314, 317, 318–19

  logo, 322, 325
  reclaimed wood doors, 322–23
  Santa Fe, 316, 317, 320, 322–23, 330
  storage and files, 320–21, 326, 330–33, 400
  swatches, 80–81, 328–29
Grand Rapids Furniture Museum, 178
graphic design, 208–10, 208–21. See also typefaces; specific restaurants, stores, and other client names
  Alphabet, 74–5, 125
  Braniff, 148, 151, 154, 157–62, 165, 210, 403
  Computer, 95, 98
  exhibitions, 186–87, 198, 200, 204–5, 218, 317, 324
  Girard's studio logos, 322, 325
  Herman Miller, 112–13, 133, 208–10, 210, 213, 220, 399
  interlocking "S" initials and names (Sandro and Susan), 15, 40, 63, 210, 211, 213–14, 217
  Names, 62, 210
  Soren residence, 290, 292

Hallmark executive apartment, 286–89, 288, 290, 400, 401
HemisFair '68. See World's Fair (San Antonio)
Herman Miller, 13, 45, 52, 53, 85, 124, 132, 148–49, 151, 156, 262, 320, 342, 381. See also Action Office; Environmental Enrichment Panels; Girard Furniture Collection; Girard Group for Herman Miller; product design; textile design; Textiles & Objects shop
  advertisement for, 57, 112–13, 133, 208–10, 210, 213, 220, 395, 399
  NYC showroom, 93, 114, 114–17, 121, 122–23, 220
  San Francisco showroom, 52, 54–55, 93, 210

Indianapolis Museum of Art, 304, 398
interior design. See residential interiors
Irwin Miller offices, 17, 258, 262, 272–73, 400, 401

Jackson Lodge, 278–79
Jayakar, Pupul, 370
John Deere, 176, 176–78, 180, 187, 400, 402
Johnson, Philip, 401
Junior League Little Shop, 258, 260–61, 394, 395

Kiley, Dan, 304, 312, 398
Knoll furniture company, 42, 52, 99, 106, 183, 317
Kouwenhoven, John A., 180, 187

La Fonda del Sol, 212, 222, 228, 236–54, 236–55, 361, 400, 401
Larsen, Jack Lenor, 18, 52, 93, 106, 142–43, 195, 210, 255, 290
Le Pavillon, 222
L'Etoile, 106, 217, 219, 221–27, 222, 228, 232, 402, 403
letterforms. See graphic design; typefaces
Longley, Bernique, 344, 373, 394

Miller, Irwin, 13, 17, 258, 304, 308, 310, 401. See also Irwin Miller offices
Miller residence, 17, 210, *211*, 304–12, *304–13*, *397*, *398*, 399
Miller, Xenia, 13, 17, 304, *307*, 308, *309*, 310, 312, 398
Moore, Henry, 308, 317
murals, 132, *176–78*, 180, 187, 222, *230–31*, 255, 260, 262, *262–64*, 265, *268–69*, 288, 290, 339, 341, *343–45*, 361, *372–73*, *376–77*, 388, 392, 394, 395, 400, 402, 403
Museum of International Folk Art, 180, *186–96*, 194, 199, 207, 218, 265, 401, 404, 405
Museum of Modern Art, 17, *178–79*, *185*, 398

Nativity scenes, 180, *204–7*, 207, *366–67*, 400, 401
Nelson Gallery, *204–7*, 207, 401
Nelson, George, 13, 106, *395*, 397–98, 405
Neuhart, Marilyn, *117*, 121
Newberry Institute of Art, 396, 397
Noguchi, Isamu, 106, 398
North Christian Church (Columbus, IN), 397
No-Sag Spring Co., 258, *270–71*, 395, 397

O'Keeffe, Georgia, 13, 38, 199, 396, 397, 399, 404

Panton, Verner, 405
Passy Restaurant, 222, 256
Pei, I. M., 39, 106, 401
Picasso, Pablo, 317
porcelains, Italian, *14*, *24–25*, 100
product design, 100–147
 archival storage boxes, 320, *320–21*, 326, 330
 beds, *105*, 283, 290, *293*, 405
 Braniff plane interiors and lounges, 106, *148*, 151, 153, *148–65*, 316, 402, *403*
 cabinets, 114, 143, *147*, 169, *182*, *261*, 278, *278–79*, 285, 290, 293, 311, *312*, 317, *354–55*, *372*, 385, 404, 405
 chairs, *100–101*, 106, *107–109*, 111, *150*, *172–73*, *183*, 232, *270–71*, 278–81, 286, 289, 309, 310, *316*, *347–49*, 360, 394
 clocks, *169*, 320, 361, *370*
 desks, 169, *173–74*, *273*, *275*, 283, 288, 289, *316*, 317, *343*, 396, 400
 Detrola, 10, 13, 45, *166–69*, *166–75*, 228, 394, *395*
 dinnerware and tableware, 25, 106, *142–43*, *143–45*, *242–45*, 254, 255, 398
 mirrors, 114, *118–19*, *343*, 393, 401
 ottomans, *104*, *107–108*, *110*, 150, *283*, *311*
 pillow slip covers, *120–21*, *304–305*, *307*, *358–59*, *364–65*
 restaurants, 222, *222–54*, *228*, *232*, *236*, 255
 sofas, 10, 106, *107*, *109*, 111, *150*, *172*, 258, 300, *312*, *337*, *339*, *342*, *350*, *360–61*, 402

 tables in business settings, *172*, *261*, *274*, *276*
 tables in home settings, 100, *306*, *308*, *311*, *342*, *347*, 360, *366*, *381*
 tabletop design, 142, *142–43*, *146–47*, *338–39*, *371*, 398, 399
 wallpapers, 124, *124–31*, 132, 398, 399
promotional materials. See graphic design; specific restaurants and businesses
Pucci, Emilio, 151, *156*

Reiss, Hilde, *178–79*
residential interiors, 278, *278–313*, 288, 290, 294, 304, 308, 310, 312. See also specific homes
restaurant design, *222*, *222–35*, *228*, *232*, *236*, *236–54*, 255, 394, 395, 400, 401, 402, 403. See also Charles' a la Pomme Soufflee; Compound; La Fonda del Sol; L'Etoile
Rieveschl residence, 294, 302, *294–303*, 398, 399
Rockefeller Center decorative arts and crafts exhibition, *11*, 256, *284–85*, 392, 393

Saarinen, Eero, 13, 17, 106, *176–77*, 180, *185*, 187, 258, 304, *304–305*, 310, 312, *318–19*, 397–98
 St. Louis Gateway Arch, 396, 397
St. John's College (Sante Fe, NM), 262, *262–67*, 400, 402
salvaged/weathered wood, *34*, *178*, *179*, *188*, 265, *268–69*, 317, *322–23*, 360, *370*, *381*, 402, 403
Scoren residence, 210, 290, *292–93*, 404, 405
sketches and sketchbooks, *19–22*, *27*, *30*, *50–51*, 98, *104–105*, *112*, *166*, *187*, *211–17*, *242*, 255, 396, 399
snake designs, *16–17*, *134*, *197*, *203*, *205*, *232*, *361*, *370*
Steinberg, Saul, 106, 302, 317

textile design, 42–99. See also Environmental Enrichment Panels
 airline seats and lounges, *85*, *148–52*, *151*, *156*, *163–64*, 403
 Alphabet, *74–75*
 Arabesque, *48–49*
 Checkers, *85*, *156*, *381*
 Computer, *95*, 98
 Crosses, *47*
 paper collage, *44*, *46*, *58*, *94*
 Dove, 99
 Eden, *64–65*
 Extrusion, *97*
 Feathers, *72–73*
 Firecracker, *68*, *262*, *274*
 Grid, *61*
 Jagged, *97*
 January, *66–67*
 Jogs, *69*
 Lace, *97*
 Links, 99
 Manhattan, *45*, *52*

 Mexicotton, *84*, *86–92*, 98, *133–41*, 405
 Mikado, *60*
 Miller Metric, *93*
 Multiform, *42–45*
 Names, *62*, 210
 Palio, *78–79*, 290, 405
 Pins, *58*
 Quatrefoil, *70–71*
 Rain, *61*
 Ribbons, *46*
 Sansusie, *63*
 Spines, *36*, 99
 stripe studies, *52*
 Super Stripe, *76–77*
 swatch books, *52*, *56–57*
 Treads, *96*
 Wire, 99
 wool stripes, *80–83*
Textiles & Objects (T&O) shop, *39*, *112–18*, *114*, *120–23*, *121*, 124, 210, 220, 400, 401
Thonet, Michael, *185*
timeline, 392–405
typefaces, *74–75*, 95, 98, *112–13*, *121*, 124, *125*, *133*, *142*, *143*, *148*, *154*, *157–62*, *165*, *186–87*, *198*, *200*, *204–5*, *207*, *208*, 210, *208–21*, 227, *235*, *238–41*, 255, *314–15*, *317*, *324*, 399, 403. See also graphic design

Unitarian Church (Albuquerque), *262–65*, *268–69*, 402, 403
Uruapan textile factory, *86*, *91*, 98

Vitra design, 405

Walker Art Center, *178–79*, *179*, *181–83*, 396, 397
Wells, Mary, 148, *153*
Wollering residence, *283*, 288
Women's Exchange Fair, *256–57*, 258, *259*, 394, 395
woodworking/wooden objects, *23*, *26–30*, *32–34*, *100–103*, *182*, *366–67*, 392, 395. See also salvaged/weathered wood
World's Fair (San Antonio, 1968), 180, 187, *190*, *198–203*, 203, *205*, 403, 405

Page numbers in *italic* refer to illustrations.

Phaidon Press Limited
2 Cooperage Yard
London E15 2QR

Phaidon Press Inc.
111 Broadway
New York, NY 10006

phaidon.com

First published 2024
© 2024 Phaidon Press Limited

ISBN 978 1 83866 759 7

A CIP catalogue record for this book is available from the British Library and the Library of Congress.

All rights reserved. No part of this publication may be reproduced, stored in a retrieval system or transmitted, in any form or by any means, electronic, mechanical, photocopying, recording or otherwise, without the written permission of Phaidon Press Limited.

Commissioning Editor: Deborah Aaronson
Project Editor: Stephanie Holstein
Production Controller: Andie Trainer
Design: Todd Oldham and Joseph Kaplan

Printed in China

Special thanks to

Tony Longoria
Deb Aaronson
Jack Oldham
Joseph Kaplan
João Mota
Julia Hasting
Stephanie Holstein
Andie Trainer
Kiera Coffee
Kori Girard
Aleishall Girard Maxon
Greg Kozatek
Georgia Smith
William Norwich
Wendy Goodman
Jenny Slate

Front Endpapers
Left: *Mexicotton Stripes*, 1961. Right: *Mexicotton Stripes*, 1961. Left: *Mexidot stripe with red check*, 1961

Frontmatter
1. Paper sun collage, 1960.
2. *Mexicotton Stripes*, 1961.
3. Woven wool sateen stripe, 1960.

Back Endpapers
Right: *Mexicotton Stripes*, 1961. Left: *Mexicotton Stripes*, 1961. Right: *Mexicotton Stripes*, 1961.

Elmer Astleford 169, 175, 260, 261, 278–79, 280, 281, 283 314–15, 318, 319

F. Barsotti 334–35, 336, 337

Bawas Friehauf Company 270

Hedrich Blessing Studio 271

Charles Eames © Eames Office, LLC. All rights reserved 8–9, 41, 42–43, 49, 55, 60, 70, 116, 117, 122, 194, 222–23, 224, 225, 226, 227, 246, 248, 249, 250–251, 284, 286, 287, 288, 289, 294–95, 296, 297, 298, 299, 300, 301, 302, 303, 366, 368, 371, 372, 373, 378, 379, 380

© Ray Eames 254 (left, top and left, bottom)

© Yale Joel / The LIFE Picture Collection / Shutterstock 247

Balthazar Korab © Library of Congress, Prints & Photographs Division, Balthazar Korab Collection 272, 273, 276, 277

© Eric Laignel 292, 293

Mark Mahaney 404 (bottom right)

© Maynard L. Parker, Courtesy of The Huntington Library, San Marino, California 351, 352, 353, 356, 357

Andrew Plotchay for Freepress 7

Frank Randt 228, 284, 285

Louis Reems 252, 253, 254 (left, middle and right, bottom)

Virginia Roehl 146

© Ezra Stoller 37, 304–5, 306, 307 (bottom), 312

Carl Ulrich 185

Jeffery White 282

Additional photographs and scans from Girard Studio and by Todd Oldham and Jason Frank Rothenberg